The Pyramid Trust: Igniting Trust in Leadership and Professional Life

Brian Bracy

Table Of Contents

Introduction..**6**

Chapter 1...**10**

Understanding Trust............................... 10

Defining Trust: Unveiling Its Multifaceted
Dimensions.. 11

Trust And The Brain: Unraveling The
Neuroscience Of Trust............................ 16

Vulnerability And Trust: The Courageous
Connection..22

Building Trust: A Two-Way Street Of Earnest
Bonds..27

Chapter 2...**34**

The Trust Crisis: Unveiling The Scarcity In Modern
Business... 34

The Toll Of Distrust: Impact On Company
Culture And Performance............................36

Learning From The Fallen: Case Studies Of
Companies Struggling With Trust.................... 41

Rekindling The Flame: Strategies To Address
The Trust Crisis.................................. 53

Chapter 3...**61**

Trust In Leadership: Guiding Lights For
Empowering Trust.................................. 61

The Leader's Crucible: Trust As The Foundation
Of Effective Leadership............................62

Trust-Building Strategies For Leaders And

Managers: Inspiring Loyalty And Respect........68

Leading By Example: Insights From Successful Leaders Who Prioritize Trust............74

Navigating The Abyss: Consequences Of A Lack Of Trust In Leadership............81

Chapter 4............**88**

Trust In Teams And Organizations: Nurturing A Culture Of Belonging............88

The Team Dynamic: Trust's Influence On Collaboration And Performance............89

Forging Authentic Connections: Fostering A Culture Of Trust In Organizations............95

Breaking Barriers: Overcoming Trust Challenges In The Workplace............101

Chapter 5............**108**

Trust In Communication And Transparency: Building Bridges Of Openness............108

Transparent Truths: The Power Of Clear Communication In Restoring Trust............109

Unraveling Deception: Addressing Rumors, Misinformation, And Corporate Secrecy............118

The Heart Of Dialogue: Creating Open Channels For Trust-Building............133

Chapter 6............**141**

The Pyramid Trust In Action: Empowering Positive Change............141

Chapter 7............**157**

Overcoming Trust Barriers: Breaking Free From Doubt And Distrust............157

The Barrier Discovery: Identifying Common Obstacles To Trust And Transformation..........158

Building Bridges: Strategies To Overcome Fear, Skepticism, And Past Experiences.................. 176

Trust In A Distrusting World: Rebuilding Faith In A Society Plagued By Distrust........................ 204

Personal Growth Through Trust: Empowering The Journey Of Self-Discovery......................214

Chapter 8..**236**

Customer Trust: The Heart Of Thriving Businesses... 236

Keeping Promises: Delivering On Commitments For Lasting Customer Relationships............... 248

Redemption Road: Rebuilding Trust After Customer Grievances.......................................257

Conclusion..**266**

INTRODUCTION

In a world filled with complexity and rapid change, there remains a timeless force that forms the bedrock of all meaningful human connections. It's a force that transcends boundaries, bridges gaps, and ignites profound transformations – the power of trust. Welcome to "The Pyramid Trust: Igniting Trust in Leadership and Professional Life"

Welcome to a transformative expedition that delves into the heart of human connections—the awe-inspiring power of trust. It is with great enthusiasm that I invite you to embark on this journey with me, where we will unravel the profound significance of trust as the cornerstone of personal and professional relationships.

In the tapestry of life, trust forms the very fabric that binds us together, weaving the threads of authenticity and vulnerability. Trust breathes life into relationships, nurturing bonds that endure the trials of time and adversity.

Yet, trust's influence transcends mere connections—it serves as the catalyst that sparks positive change and transformation. The chapters that follow will unveil the remarkable ways trust empowers us to grow, to embrace resilience, and to embrace a world where endless possibilities await.

With each revelation, we'll immerse ourselves in the concept of the "The Pyramid Trust," a phenomenon that ignites a wave of transformation. Witness how trust's influence ripples across our lives, touching hearts, and leaving an indelible impact on individuals, relationships, and society at large.

Throughout this journey, you will become the architect of change, empowered to harness the immense potential of trust in your own life. Whether in personal connections or professional endeavors, The Pyramid Trust knows no boundaries—it transforms and elevates us beyond our expectations.

Yet, this journey is not one of despair but of hope and resilience. It is a journey where we explore the transformative power of trust in business relationships, even after facing betrayal, and learn to nurture trust in a society plagued by doubt and skepticism.

So, buckle up as we embark on an exploration of The Pyramid Trust and unleash the potential within ourselves to create a world of authentic connections and unwavering belief. Together, let us kindle the flame of transformation and embrace the power of trust to shape a future filled with limitless possibilities.

Are you ready to dive into this profound journey of trust, connection, and transformation? Let the voyage begin.

CHAPTER 1

UNDERSTANDING TRUST

Trust is a pivotal thread that binds us together in the intricate tapestry of human relationships. As we embark on our quest to explore the depths of trust, we delve into the heart of this enigmatic force, seeking to unveil its many facets and unravel the intricate web it weaves.

This chapter sets the stage for understanding trust – from its definition and neuroscience to the delicate dance of vulnerability and the art of building earnest bonds. Join us as we unlock the mysteries of trust and lay the foundation for transformative connections that transcend time and space.

DEFINING TRUST: UNVEILING ITS MULTIFACETED DIMENSIONS

In the intricate landscape of human emotions and interactions, trust is an intangible pillar supporting the foundation of our relationships. Trust is a delicate dance of vulnerability and belief, a complex interplay of emotions and judgments that shapes our connections with others and ourselves.

- **Trust as the Bedrock of Connections:**

At its simplest, trust can be described as the bedrock upon which all meaningful relationships are built. The invisible force allows us to let down our guard, enabling genuine connections and fostering intimacy. Trust forms the basis of friendships, love, and partnerships and is the cornerstone of thriving professional relationships in the workplace. When trust is present, walls come down, and bridges are built, forging bonds that withstand the tests of time and adversity.

- **The Dual Nature of Trust:**

Trust exists in a dual nature, intertwining its manifestations in the external world and the internal landscape of our minds. Externally, trust is an act of vulnerability, where we place our faith in others' intentions, actions, and promises. It is the belief that they will act in our best interest, uphold their commitments, and safeguard our well-being.

Internally, trust is an emotional and cognitive assessment that evaluates perceived reliability, competence, and benevolence. A delicate balance of intuition and reasoning guides our decisions to extend or withhold trust in different situations and individuals.

- **The Gradations of Trust:**

Trust is not a monolithic concept but an intricate spectrum with varying degrees and gradations. At one end lies complete trust, where unwavering faith is bestowed upon another, and at the other, complete distrust, where suspicion and skepticism take root.

Between these extremes are varying levels of trust, influenced by past experiences, cultural norms, and individual predispositions. Understanding the nuances of trust's gradations helps us navigate its complexities and adapt our approach in different contexts.

- **Trust and Vulnerability:**

Central to trust's nature is the profound connection it shares with vulnerability. Trust requires us to lower our defenses, making ourselves susceptible to potential harm or disappointment. It is a courageous act of vulnerability, exposing our innermost hopes, fears, and desires to others. However, trust is a two-way street; when reciprocated, it creates a safe space for mutual vulnerability, strengthening the fabric of our relationships and fostering a sense of belonging.

- **Trust and Accountability:**

Trust is not blind faith; it is built on a foundation of accountability. Trustworthy individuals and organizations take responsibility for their actions, acknowledge mistakes, and demonstrate transparency.

Accountability nurtures trust, showing a willingness to rectify errors and restore faith when trust has been challenged or breached.

Without accountability, trust falters, and the connection threads begin to unravel.

- **The Contextual Nature of Trust:**

Trust is inherently contextual, shaped by unique circumstances, cultural norms, and individual experiences. What engenders trust in one situation or relationship might not hold the same weight in another. It is essential to recognize the contextual nature of trust to avoid generalizations and understand the nuanced factors that influence its dynamics.

In our pursuit to define trust, we discover that it is more than a mere word in our vocabulary – it is an intricate dance of vulnerability and belief woven into the fabric of our lives. As we proceed on our journey to explore trust's profound impact on our brains, emotions, and relationships, we gain deeper insights into the power it wields and the transformative potential it holds.

TRUST AND THE BRAIN: UNRAVELING THE NEUROSCIENCE OF TRUST

- **The Trust Circuitry: Building Bridges in the Brain**

Trust is not solely a matter of the heart but also a product of the brain's intricate circuitry. Within the neural architecture, specific regions play pivotal roles in processing trust-related information. The amygdala, responsible for emotional processing, is a crucial player, scanning for potential threats or indicators of trustworthiness in others' actions and expressions.

On the other hand, the prefrontal cortex, associated with higher-order cognitive functions, evaluates this information, making calculated judgments about whether to extend trust or exercise caution.

- **Oxytocin: The Neurochemical Elixir of Trust**

At the heart of the neuroscience of trust lies the remarkable hormone oxytocin – often dubbed the "love hormone" or "bonding hormone." Released in response to social interactions, particularly those marked by trust and intimacy, oxytocin plays a crucial role in forging and strengthening human connections.

This neurochemical elixir promotes prosocial behaviors, fosters empathy, and cultivates feelings of warmth and attachment, acting as a powerful catalyst for trust between individuals.

- **Trust and the Mirror Neuron System**

Our brains are equipped with a fascinating mechanism called the mirror neuron system, which enables us to experience a form of empathetic resonance with others. When we observe someone engaging in trustworthy behaviors, such as acts of kindness or honesty, our mirror neurons fire, mirroring those actions in our neural patterns. This mirroring process fosters a sense of connection and empathy, developing trust and strengthening social bonds.

- **Early Life Experiences: The Foundation of Trust**

The roots of trust can often be traced back to our early life experiences and the quality of our attachment to primary caregivers. Secure attachment during infancy lays a sturdy foundation for developing trust in future relationships, instilling a sense of safety, predictability, and emotional responsiveness. Conversely, early experiences of neglect or inconsistency may lead to challenges in forming and maintaining trust in adulthood.

- **Neuroplasticity and Trust: The Power of Rewiring**

The human brain is remarkably adaptive, constantly reshaping its neural pathways in response to experiences. This neuroplasticity offers hope for those who struggle with trust issues, as it means that new trust pathways can be forged with deliberate effort and positive experiences.

By consciously engaging in trustworthy actions and surrounding oneself with supportive individuals, it is possible to rewire the brain and foster a greater capacity for trust.

- **The Dark Side of Trust: Betrayal and Its Neural Impact**

While trust is a transformative force, it's dark counterpart – betrayal – can profoundly impact the brain. Betrayal activates areas of the brain associated with emotional pain, triggering feelings of hurt, anger, and a reluctance to trust again. Understanding the neural mechanisms at play in trust and betrayal sheds light on the complexity of these emotions. It paves the way for healing and growth.

- **Building a Trustful Brain: Practices for Cultivating Trust**

Just as trust shapes the brain, the brain also shapes trust. By engaging in mindfulness practices, cultivating self-compassion, and intentionally fostering positive social interactions, you will nurture a trustful brain that leans towards openness and connection. These practices empower you to navigate the delicate dance of trust with heightened awareness and resilience.

As we unravel the neuroscience of trust, we are met with a profound revelation – trust is not solely a product of our emotions but a fascinating interplay between neurobiology and social dynamics.

By gaining insights into how trust is wired in our brains, we open doors to a deeper understanding and appreciation of this intricate force that binds us together. Join us as we continue to explore the profound impact of trust in various domains of life and uncover the transformative potential it holds in fostering authentic connections and facilitating positive change.

VULNERABILITY AND TRUST: THE COURAGEOUS CONNECTION

In the tapestry of trust, vulnerability emerges as an essential thread, weaving together the fabric of genuine connections. At the heart of trust lies the courageous act of vulnerability – the willingness to expose our true selves, fears, and imperfections to others.

- **The Paradox of Vulnerability:**

Vulnerability is often misunderstood as a sign of weakness, but paradoxically, it requires tremendous strength and courage. To be vulnerable means to acknowledge and share our uncertainties, insecurities, and emotions with others, exposing us to rejection or judgment. It is the act of stepping into the unknown, relinquishing control and embracing the uncertainty that lies at the heart of authentic trust.

- **Vulnerability in Leadership:**

In the realm of leadership, vulnerability takes on a unique significance. Leaders who embrace vulnerability are perceived as more authentic and relatable, fostering robust team bonds. Sharing personal stories of challenges and growth allows you to connect on a human level, inspiring trust and loyalty. Vulnerability in leadership also encourages team members to feel safe in expressing their ideas and concerns, leading to a more collaborative and innovative work environment.

- **The Healing Power of Vulnerability:**

Vulnerability can be a potent agent of healing in relationships that have experienced breaches of trust. When you are willing to be vulnerable and express remorse for past actions, it opens the door to forgiveness and reconciliation—rebuilding trust after a betrayal often necessitates vulnerability and transparency, demonstrating a commitment to growth and positive change.

- **Navigating Fear and Resistance:**

Embracing vulnerability can be challenging, as fear and resistance may arise. Fear of judgment, rejection, or emotional pain can hinder individuals from being fully open and authentic.

Understanding these fears and recognizing their origins is crucial to overcoming them. Cultivating self-compassion and seeking support from trusted individuals will help navigate the emotional barriers to vulnerability.

- **Trusting Ourselves: The First Step to Trusting Others:**

To trust others, we must first trust ourselves – our instincts, judgments, and ability to navigate vulnerability. Self-trust serves as a solid foundation upon which we build trust in others. When you believe in your capacity to handle vulnerability outcomes, you are more likely to take the courageous step toward trusting others.

- **Vulnerability and Growth:**

In vulnerability, there is the potential for growth and self-discovery. By embracing vulnerability, we allow ourselves to confront our fears, acknowledge our limitations, and open ourselves to new experiences. The act of vulnerability becomes an empowering journey of personal growth, paving the way for greater resilience and authenticity.

As we explore the courageous connection between vulnerability and trust, we discover that vulnerability is not a sign of weakness but a profound testament to our strength and authenticity. It is a journey of self-acceptance and courage, leading to transformative connections and deepening trust in our relationships.

BUILDING TRUST: A TWO-WAY STREET OF EARNEST BONDS

Trust is a precious currency in human interactions, cultivated through earnest efforts and genuine intentions. Building trust is a dynamic process akin to navigating a two-way street, where both parties play integral roles in forging and nurturing the bonds that form the foundation of authentic connections. Now, we will explore the art and science of building trust, uncovering the key elements that contribute to its growth, and understanding the reciprocity required for its sustenance.

- **The Trust Building Blocks:**

Trust is constructed brick by brick, requiring a careful alignment of intentions, actions, and character. Transparent communication, reliability, and consistent follow-through are essential trust-building blocks that underpin any relationship. By consistently demonstrating these qualities, individuals create a solid groundwork upon which trust can thrive.

- **Authenticity: The Keystone of Trust:**

At the heart of building trust lies authenticity – the genuine expression of one's true self and intentions. Authenticity fosters a sense of transparency, allowing others to see and connect with the real person behind the façade. When you consistently show up as your true selves, you inspire trust in others, as authenticity breeds trust like no other trait.

- **Empathy and Active Listening:**

The art of building trust requires the practice of empathy and active listening. The ability to understand and share the feelings of another, creating a sense of emotional connection and validation is empathy. On the other hand, active listening involves fully engaging in the conversation without judgment or interruption, allowing the other person to feel heard and valued. These practices deepen understanding, strengthen connections, and foster an environment of trust.

- **Consistency: The Bridge to Reliability:** Trust cannot flourish in an atmosphere of unpredictability. Consistency in words, actions, and reliability builds a bridge individuals can cross with confidence, knowing they will encounter consistency and dependability on the other side. Being consistent in good times and challenging moments nurtures trust and cements individual bonds.

- **Vulnerability: The Gateway to Deeper Trust:**

Vulnerability plays a vital role in trust-building. When individuals demonstrate vulnerability, they signal to others that they are willing to take risks and share their authentic selves. This courageous act invites reciprocity, fostering deeper trust and openness.

- **Transparency and Honesty:**

Transparency and honesty are cornerstones of trust-building. Individuals who are open and truthful in their communication create an atmosphere of trust where there are no hidden agendas or deceitful intentions. Trust flourishes when there is a mutual understanding that both parties prioritize transparency and honesty.

- **Accountability and Repairing Trust:** Building trust is an ongoing process that requires accountability. When trust is breached, whether through mistakes or misunderstandings, taking responsibility and making amends is essential for repairing the trust bond. Owning up to errors and committing to positive change demonstrates integrity and reinforces trust-building.

- **Patience and Time:** Trust cannot be rushed; it requires patience and time to grow and deepen. Building trust is a gradual process that unfolds through shared experiences, consistent interactions, and deepening emotional connections. Recognizing that trust is an evolving journey helps individuals appreciate the value of the bonds they cultivate.

- **Cultural and Contextual Sensitivity:**
Building trust in diverse contexts and cultural settings demands sensitivity and adaptability. Understanding and respecting cultural norms and communication styles is crucial for building trust across different backgrounds and experiences.

- **Trust as a Shared Responsibility:**
In the realm of trust, both parties bear responsibility for its cultivation and maintenance. Trust is a reciprocal process that thrives when both individuals actively contribute to the growth and sustenance of the relationship.

As we explore the intricacies of building trust as a two-way street, we recognize that trust is not a static destination but an ongoing journey of mutual investment and vulnerability. A dance of authenticity, empathy, consistency, and accountability shapes the bonds that connect us.

CHAPTER 2

THE TRUST CRISIS: UNVEILING THE SCARCITY IN MODERN BUSINESS

In the dynamic landscape of modern business, trust is a vital currency that fuels growth, fosters collaboration and propels success. Yet, in recent times, a haunting specter has emerged – the trust crisis.

As we step into Chapter 3, we confront the harsh reality of this scarcity of trust that pervades the corporate world. This chapter unveils the profound impact of the trust crisis on company culture, employee morale, and overall business performance.

We delve deep into the root causes of this crisis and learn invaluable lessons from real-life case studies of companies that have grappled with the consequences of diminishing trust.

Do not take trust for granted as you unravel the trust crisis in modern business; you are confronted with this sobering reality. It is a fragile yet essential pillar supporting thriving organizations' edifice. Join us as we venture into the heart of the trust crisis, examining its repercussions and discovering the transformative potential of rebuilding trust to pursue a resilient, trust-filled corporate future.

THE TOLL OF DISTRUST: IMPACT ON COMPANY CULTURE AND PERFORMANCE

In the ever-evolving landscape of modern business, trust is the lifeblood that sustains healthy company culture and drives peak performance. However, when the delicate threads of trust unravel, a pervasive sense of distrust takes root, casting a long shadow over every aspect of an organization. This chapter delves into the profound toll of distrust on company culture and performance, exploring its multifaceted impact on employees, leadership, and overall business success.

- **The Erosion of Company Culture:**

Company culture, often called the "heartbeat" of an organization, is deeply affected by distrust. In an environment tainted by suspicion and lack of faith, employee morale plummets, and disengagement prevails. Collaboration and teamwork suffer as individuals become guarded, fearing hidden agendas and a lack of transparency. The once vibrant and inclusive culture becomes fragmented, hindering the organization's ability to unite behind a shared vision.

- **The Decline in Employee Motivation:**

Trust is a fundamental driver of employee motivation.

Employees who perceive a lack of trust from their superiors or peers may feel undervalued and disempowered. The resulting decline in motivation hampers creativity and innovation, leaving employees hesitant to take risks or propose new ideas. In contrast, organizations that foster a culture of trust inspire you to take initiative, innovate, and invest wholeheartedly in their work.

- **Impact on Communication and Collaboration:**

Distrust casts a veil of uncertainty over communication channels, hindering open and honest dialogue. Employees may withhold valuable insights or hesitate to express concerns, fearing repercussions. The breakdown of communication stifles collaboration and prevents the organization from harnessing the collective wisdom of its workforce. Effective teamwork and problem-solving become elusive; hidden agendas and self-interest may cloud decision-making processes.

- **Loss of Employee Loyalty and Commitment:**

Trust is the glue that binds employees to an organization, fostering a sense of loyalty and commitment. When trust is eroded, employees may question your allegiance to the organization. High turnover rates and increased employee churn become evident as disheartened employees seek opportunities elsewhere. This loss of loyalty impacts the retention of valuable talent. Also, it incurs significant costs associated with recruiting and onboarding new employees.

- **Impact on Leadership Effectiveness:**

In an environment of distrust, leadership effectiveness is profoundly compromised—leaders perceived as untrustworthy struggle to inspire and motivate your teams. Trust is necessary to maintain the credibility of leaders' vision and strategic decisions, making it challenging to rally employees behind a shared purpose. Effective leadership requires a foundation of trust, as leaders who lead with integrity and authenticity foster a culture of trust and engender loyalty in their teams.

- **Implications for Business Performance:** Ultimately, the toll of distrust on company culture and employee performance cascades into broader implications for overall business performance. Decreased employee productivity, lower levels of innovation, and increased absenteeism contribute to reduced operational efficiency and financial losses. Additionally, the negative impact on customer relationships and brand reputation can lead to declining customer loyalty and market share.

- **Addressing the Distrust Paradox:**

Breaking free from distrust is challenging but essential for organizations seeking sustainable success. Acknowledging the paradox that rebuilding trust requires trust is a critical first step. Transparent communication, consistent actions, and a commitment to accountability are crucial elements in rebuilding trust. As a leader, you must lead by example, demonstrating trustworthiness and fostering a culture of open dialogue and collaboration.

LEARNING FROM THE FALLEN: CASE STUDIES OF COMPANIES STRUGGLING WITH TRUST

Within the annals of corporate history, cautionary tales exist of companies grappling with trust issues, leading to high-profile scandals, organizational breakdowns, and reputational damage.Now, we will draw invaluable lessons from the fall, and uncover the common pitfalls that can lead to a trust crisis within organizations.

- **Enron Corporation: The Specter of Deceit**

One of the most infamous cases of a trust crisis is the Enron Corporation, which once stood as an emblem of corporate success before its shocking downfall. The Enron scandal was a culmination of fraudulent accounting practices, deceitful reporting, and a lack of transparency at the highest levels of the company. This case study is a stark reminder of the dire consequences of compromised trust and the need for transparency and ethical leadership.

- **Volkswagen: Emissions Scandal and Betrayal of Trust**

A renowned automobile manufacturer, Volkswagen faced a trust crisis when it was revealed that the company had deliberately manipulated emissions data to meet regulatory standards. The "dieselgate" scandal resulted in significant financial penalties and loss of public trust. This case study highlights the damaging impact of betraying the trust of customers and the public, underscoring the importance of ethical practices and honest communication.

- **Wells Fargo: Betrayal of Customers' Trust**

Wells Fargo, a major banking institution, faced a trust crisis when it was discovered that employees had opened millions of unauthorized accounts to meet aggressive sales targets. The scandal revealed a culture prioritizing short-term profits over customer trust and ethical conduct. This case study emphasizes the need for organizations to prioritize customers' best interests and maintain integrity in their business practices.

- **Theranos: The Illusion of Innovation**

Theranos, a once-celebrated healthcare startup, promised revolutionary blood-testing technology but faced a trust crisis when it became evident that the technology needed to deliver on its claims. The company's leadership misrepresented the capabilities of the technology and withheld critical information from investors and the public. This case study highlights the importance of honesty and transparency when making claims about products or services.

- **Uber: Cultural Failures and Breach of Trust**

Uber, a pioneering ride-sharing company, faced a trust crisis due to cultural failures, including allegations of sexual harassment and a lack of accountability at the executive level. The company's tarnished reputation led to losing trust among employees, customers, and investors. This case study illustrates the significance of building a culture of trust and fostering an environment where employees feel safe and valued.

- **Facebook: Data Privacy Breaches and Trust Erosion**

Facebook, a social media giant, faced multiple trust crises related to data privacy breaches and mishandling of user data. The Cambridge

Analytica scandal, in particular, exposed the vulnerability of user information and led to widespread concerns about data privacy. This case study underscores the need for organizations to prioritize the protection of user data and be transparent about data usage.

- **Toshiba: Accounting Scandal and Integrity Compromises**

Toshiba, a prominent Japanese conglomerate, faced a trust crisis when it was revealed that the company had engaged in accounting irregularities to inflate profits. The scandal severely damaged the company's reputation and led to significant financial losses. This case study highlights the importance of maintaining financial integrity and ethical conduct in corporate practices.

- **Boeing: Safety Concerns and Stakeholder Mistrust**

Boeing, a renowned aircraft manufacturer, faced a trust crisis following two deadly crashes involving its 737 Max aircraft.

Questions were raised about the company's safety procedures and regulatory oversight. The crisis led to a loss of trust among passengers, airlines, and regulators. This case study underscores the critical role of prioritizing safety and maintaining open communication with stakeholders.

Learning from these fallen companies provides essential lessons for organizations seeking to avoid a trust crisis. Transparent leadership, ethical practices, a culture of accountability, and a commitment to customer and stakeholder trust are essential elements in building and maintaining a strong foundation of trust.

Uncovering the common pitfalls that can lead to a trust crisis within organizations is crucial for proactive trust-building and maintaining a healthy work environment. Here are some common pitfalls to be aware of:

1. **Lack of Transparency:** When organizations lack transparency in their actions, decisions, and communication, employees may feel left in the dark, leading to suspicion and mistrust.

2. **Inconsistent Communication:** Poor or inconsistent communication can create misunderstandings and uncertainty among

employees, eroding trust in leadership and the organization as a whole.

3. **Broken Promises:** Failing to deliver on promises and commitments can damage trust and credibility, making employees hesitant to trust future assurances.

4. **Micromanagement:** Excessive micromanagement can signal a lack of trust in employees' abilities, leading to disengagement and a breakdown of trust.

5. **Unfair Treatment:** When employees perceive favoritism or unfair treatment, it can create a toxic environment where trust in leadership and colleagues diminishes.

6. **Lack of Empathy:** Organizations that do not prioritize empathy and understanding may struggle to build authentic connections with employees, leading to a lack of trust and loyalty.

7. **Blame and Finger-Pointing:** A culture of blame and finger-pointing can discourage open communication and problem-solving, eroding trust and collaboration.

8. **Ignoring Employee Feedback:** Disregarding or dismissing employee feedback can foster a sense of insignificance and lack of trust in the organization's commitment to improvement.

9. **Ethical Lapses:** Any ethical misconduct or violation of values can severely damage trust both internally and externally, affecting the organization's reputation and relationships.

10. **Lack of Accountability:** A lack of accountability for actions or decisions can erode trust in leadership's ability to take responsibility for outcomes.

11. **Fear of Retaliation:** If employees fear retaliation for speaking up or expressing concerns, they may choose to remain silent, hindering open communication and trust-building.

12. **High Turnover Rates:** Frequent turnover can lead to a sense of instability and

uncertainty, making it difficult to build and maintain trust among employees.

13. Inconsistent Leadership Behavior: When leaders do not align their words with their actions, it can create confusion and distrust among employees.

14. Resistance to Change: If organizations resist necessary changes or fail to involve employees in decision-making processes, trust in leadership's intentions may diminish.

15. Lack of Employee Development: Neglecting employee development and growth opportunities can lead to a perception of unimportance and mistrust.

Addressing these pitfalls requires a proactive approach, emphasizing open communication, accountability, empathy, and transparency throughout the organization. Trust-building should be an ongoing effort, with leaders leading by example and fostering a culture that values trust as a cornerstone of success.

REKINDLING THE FLAME: STRATEGIES TO ADDRESS THE TRUST CRISIS

In the wake of a trust crisis, organizations stand at a crossroads – a pivotal moment where the flames of trust may flicker but, with concerted efforts, can be rekindled. Let's embark on a transformative journey, exploring strategies organizations can adopt to address the trust crisis and foster a trust, transparency, and integrity culture.

- **Transparent Leadership: Leading by Example**

Addressing the trust crisis starts at the top – with transparent and ethical leadership. You must lead by example, demonstrating honesty, accountability, and transparency in your decision-making and communication. Transparent leadership creates an environment where employees feel valued, informed, and empowered, fostering trust and loyalty.

- **Open and Honest Communication: The Foundation of Trust**

Effective communication is a linchpin in rebuilding trust. You must prioritize open and honest communication at all levels, encouraging employees to express their concerns, ideas, and feedback without fear of retribution. Transparent communication helps dispel rumors and misunderstandings, bridging the gap between leaders and employees and fostering a culture of trust.

- **Consistency and Reliability: Rebuilding Trust Brick by Brick**

Rebuilding trust requires consistent and reliable actions. You must follow through on commitments and promises, demonstrating integrity and dependability. As trust is rebuilt brick by brick, you must show your commitment to positive change through sustained, consistent efforts.

- **Accountability and Ownership: Learning from Mistakes**

Owning up to past mistakes is a crucial step in addressing the trust crisis. Organizations must take accountability for missteps and demonstrate a commitment to making amends and learning from the past. Accountability is a powerful change driver, signaling to stakeholders that the organization is dedicated to rebuilding trust.

- **Engaging Employees: Empowering Through Participation**

Empowering employees through participation and involvement in decision-making processes can contribute to rebuilding trust. When employees feel that their voices are heard and that they play a meaningful role in shaping the organization's direction, they are more likely to invest in the company's success and feel a sense of ownership and loyalty.

- **Investing in Employee Well-Being: Nurturing Trust Through Care**

Caring for the well-being of employees is an essential aspect of rebuilding trust. Organizations must prioritize employee wellness, providing support and resources to help employees navigate challenges and maintain work-life balance. A caring and supportive environment fosters a sense of trust and loyalty among employees.

- **Transparent Governance and Ethical Practices: Regaining Stakeholder Confidence**

You must institute transparent governance and adhere to ethical practices to address the trust crisis. Demonstrating a commitment to accountability, compliance, and responsible business practices is instrumental in regaining the confidence of stakeholders and rebuilding trust.

- **Embracing Diversity and Inclusion: Building a Trustful, Inclusive Culture**

Inclusive organizations that embrace diversity foster trust among employees and stakeholders by valuing and respecting different perspectives and experiences; organizations create an environment where all individuals feel included and valued. Inclusive cultures are more likely to attract and retain a diverse talent pool and inspire trust in the broader community.

- **External Validation and Independent Auditing: Restoring Confidence**

Seeking external validation through independent auditing and certifications can help restore confidence in an organization. Independent assessments of ethical practices and governance assure stakeholders that the organization is committed to transparency and integrity.

- **Patience and Long-Term Vision: Nurturing Trustful Roots**

Rebuilding trust takes time; it requires patience and a long-term vision. It would be best if you were prepared for incremental progress and setbacks along the way—nurture trust through sustained efforts with a commitment to maintaining integrity and transparency for the long haul.

As we explore the strategies to address the trust crisis, we recognize that rebuilding trust is a challenging but essential journey if you seek sustainable success. By embracing transparent leadership, prioritizing open communication,

and demonstrating accountability, you can
rekindle the flame of trust and ignite positive
change.

CHAPTER 3

TRUST IN LEADERSHIP: GUIDING LIGHTS FOR EMPOWERING TRUST

Effective leadership lies in the heart of every thriving organization, serving as a guiding light that illuminates the path to trust and success. Chapter four delves into the critical role of trust in leadership, exploring how you will become catalysts for fostering trust and authenticity within your teams and organizations. Join us as we unravel the profound impact of trustworthy leadership, revealing strategies and insights to inspire loyalty, collaboration, and transformative growth through the power of trust.

The Leader's Crucible: Trust as the Foundation of Effective Leadership

In the crucible of leadership, trust emerges as the bedrock upon which effective leadership is built. Trust is the invisible force that binds you to your teams, inspiring loyalty, collaboration, and unwavering commitment. Let's explore the pivotal role of trust in leadership, delving into the characteristics that make leaders trustworthy and the transformative impact trust has on teams and organizations.

- **The Essence of Trust in Leadership:**

Trust in leadership is not merely a desirable quality; it is an essential attribute that underpins a leader's ability to influence, motivate, and empower your team. Trusted leaders are perceived as reliable, honest, and competent, creating an atmosphere of psychological safety where team members feel secure in taking risks and expressing their ideas

.

- **Trust as a Currency of Influence:**

Effective leaders recognize that trust is a currency of influence. The trust they earn from their team members and stakeholders empowers them to inspire change, drive performance, and make critical decisions with the support of those they lead. A leader's ability to influence and lead effectively becomes severely compromised without trust.

- **Building Trust:**

    Mere words do not bestow trust in leadership; it is earned through consistent actions that align with the leader's values and intentions. Leaders must demonstrate integrity, accountability, and transparency in their decisions and interactions. By walking the talk, leaders cultivate an environment of trust where team members feel confident in the leader's authenticity and commitment.

- **Trust and Emotional Intelligence:**

Emotional intelligence is a fundamental aspect of building trust in leadership. Leaders who possess emotional intelligence are adept at understanding and managing their emotions and those of their team members. This empathetic and compassionate approach creates a sense of trust and emotional safety, where team members feel seen, heard, and valued.

- **Trust and Vulnerability:**

While leaders are often expected to exude strength and confidence, embracing vulnerability can be powerful in building trust. If you are willing to acknowledge your limitations, admit mistakes, and seek feedback, it will inspire trust in your authenticity and humility. Vulnerability fosters genuine connections, paving the way for open communication and mutual trust.

- **Trust and Decision-Making:**

The foundation of trust in leadership extends to the decision-making process. If you involve your team members in decision-making, solicit their input and consider diverse perspectives you will create a culture of trust and inclusivity. This participatory approach not only fosters ownership but also leads to better-informed decisions.

- **Trust as a Catalyst for Employee Engagement:**

Trust is a powerful catalyst for employee engagement. When team members trust their leaders, they are more likely to feel invested in the organization's goals, committed to their roles, and inspired to go the extra mile. Trustful leadership enhances job satisfaction and reduces employee turnover, contributing to a positive work culture.

- **The Impact of Trust on Organizational Performance:**

Trust in leadership has a direct impact on organizational performance. Trustful leaders foster high levels of collaboration, effective teamwork, and a willingness to embrace change. **So be trustful.** These attributes contribute to improved productivity, innovation, and overall business success.

- **Rebuilding Trust: The Path to Redemption:**

Leaders who have faced trust challenges have the opportunity to rebuild trust through consistent actions and a commitment to positive change. Acknowledging past mistakes, taking accountability, and demonstrating a renewed focus on transparency and integrity can pave the path to redemption and regaining trust.

- **Trust in Times of Crisis:**

In times of crisis, trust in leadership becomes even more critical. You must be able to navigate challenges with transparency, empathy, and decisiveness inspire confidence in your ability to lead the organization through turbulent waters.

Trust becomes the anchor that steadies the ship during turbulent times.

TRUST-BUILDING STRATEGIES FOR LEADERS AND MANAGERS: INSPIRING LOYALTY AND RESPECT

In leadership and management, trust stands as the linchpin that unlocks the full potential of teams and fosters a culture of loyalty and respect. Strategies that leaders and managers can employ to inspire unwavering loyalty and respect from their team members include:

- **Leading by Example: Authenticity Breeds Trust**

Effective leaders understand that trust begins with leading by example. You must inspire trust in your authenticity and integrity by embodying the values and behaviors you wish to see in your team members. Leaders who consistently align their actions with their words create a sense of psychological safety, where team members feel secure in being their authentic selves.

- **Active Listening and Empathy: Fostering Meaningful Connections**

Trust-building hinges on the art of active listening and empathy. If you genuinely listen to your team members, show understanding, and respond with empathy you will build strong emotional connections. Empathetic leaders are attuned to their team's needs, concerns, and aspirations, which fosters trust and respect within the team.

- **Transparency and Open Communication: Building Trust Through Honesty**

Transparent communication is a cornerstone of trust-building. Leaders who share information openly, even in challenging circumstances, foster trust and respect. Transparent leaders address concerns directly, providing clarity and instilling confidence in their decisions.

- **Setting Clear Expectations: Empowering Through Clarity**

Clear communication of expectations and goals empowers team members to perform their best. Leaders who provide clear guidelines and constructively offer feedback create an environment where team members feel supported and understood. The clarity in expectations fosters trust and respect in the leader's ability to guide the team toward success.

- **Accountability and Acknowledgment: Recognizing Efforts and Contributions**

This is pivotal in building trust. Leaders who celebrate successes and take accountability for mistakes create a culture of trust and respect. Acknowledgment not only motivates team members but also reinforces the trust they have in you.

- **Empowering Decision-Making: Trusting Team Members' Capabilities**

Empowering team members with decision-making responsibilities signals trust in their abilities and expertise. Leaders who delegate authority and trust their team members to make informed decisions foster a sense of ownership and respect. This approach encourages initiative and innovation within the team.

- **Building Personal Connections: Humanizing Leadership**

Trust thrives in an environment where leaders cultivate personal connections with their team members. You should humanize your role by showing genuine interest in your team members well-being and aspirations, making them feel valued and respected as individuals.

- **Consistency and Predictability: Building Reliability**

Consistency in actions and decision-making is essential in trust-building. Leaders who demonstrate reliability in their behavior create a sense of security and predictability within the team. Team members know what to expect from their leaders, which enhances trust and respect.

- **Encouraging Growth and Development: Investing in Team Members**

Investing in the growth and development of team members demonstrates trust in their potential. Leaders who provide opportunities for learning and advancement foster a sense of loyalty and respect. Team members are more likely to stay committed to an organization that invests in their professional development.

- **Resolving Conflict with Grace: Nurturing Trust in Challenging Times**

Conflict is an inevitable part of any team dynamic. Leaders who handle conflicts with grace, fairness, and respect contribute to a culture of trust. Conflict resolution based on open communication and a focus on solutions builds trust and strengthens team cohesion.

As leaders and managers adopt these trust-building strategies, they create a harmonious and high-performing environment where loyalty and respect thrive. By fostering authentic connections and empowering their teams, leaders unleash the full potential of their organizations and ignite a collective commitment to shared success.

LEADING BY EXAMPLE: INSIGHTS FROM SUCCESSFUL LEADERS WHO PRIORITIZE TRUST

Leading by example is a time-honored leadership approach that transcends cultural and organizational boundaries. Successful leaders recognize that trust is the foundation for building extraordinary teams and organizations. This chapter explores insights from remarkable leaders who prioritize trust as a guiding principle in their leadership journey. By examining their strategies, actions, and philosophies, we gain invaluable lessons on how leading by example fosters a culture of trust, loyalty, and unwavering commitment.

- **Integrity and Authenticity: A Leader's North Star**

Leaders who prioritize trust understand that integrity and authenticity are the cornerstones of their leadership. These leaders build a trustful and transparent environment by remaining true to their values and consistently aligning their actions with their words. Team members are inspired by leaders who walk the talk, fostering a sense of trust in the leader's intentions and decision-making.

- **Humility and Vulnerability: The Power of Human Connection**

Successful leaders embrace humility and vulnerability as sources of strength. Acknowledging your limitations and admitting mistakes not only humanize you but also create an environment where team members feel comfortable sharing their vulnerabilities; this fosters a deeper human connection and an atmosphere of trust and psychological safety.

- **Listening with Empathy: Fostering Meaningful Engagement**

Insightful leaders prioritize active listening with empathy. By understanding your team members' perspectives, concerns, and aspirations, these leaders demonstrate genuine care and respect. Empathetic listening builds trust, as team members feel valued and understood.

- **Transparency and Open Communication: Building Trust Through Honesty**

Leading by example includes practicing transparent and open communication. Successful leaders prioritize sharing information openly, even when discussing difficult topics. Transparent communication enhances trust, as team members know they can rely on you to be forthcoming and honest.

- **Accountability and Ownership: Taking Responsibility**

Leaders who lead by example take accountability for their decisions and actions.

They embrace ownership of successes and failures, inspiring trust in their commitment to making things right. Team members respect leaders willing to learn from and grow from their mistakes.

- **Empowering Others: Trusting in the Team's Abilities**

Empowering team members is a hallmark of leaders who prioritize trust. These leaders trust their team's capabilities and provide the autonomy to make decisions and take the initiative. Empowerment fosters a culture of trust where team members feel trusted and respected.

- **Celebrating Success and Recognizing Efforts: Inspiring Loyalty**

Successful leaders take the time to celebrate team successes and recognize individual efforts.

By acknowledging achievements, you will show appreciation for your team's hard work, motivating continued dedication and loyalty.

- **Consistency and Reliability: Building a Foundation of Trust**

Consistency in leadership actions is essential to building trust. Reliable and predictable leaders create a sense of security and stability within the team. Team members trust you when you consistently demonstrate an unwavering commitment to your values and vision.

- **Resilience in Challenging Times: Navigating Adversity**

Leading by example involves demonstrating resilience and composure during challenging times. Successful leaders remain composed under pressure and navigate adversity with grace and determination. Your resilience inspires trust in your ability to lead through uncertainty.

- **Empathy and Support: Putting People First**

Leaders who prioritize trust understand the importance of putting people first. These leaders create a caring and nurturing environment by showing empathy and providing support. Team members trust leaders who prioritize their well-being and professional growth.

By embracing integrity, vulnerability, empathy, and empowerment, you will foster a culture of trust that permeates every aspect of their organization.

NAVIGATING THE ABYSS: CONSEQUENCES OF A LACK OF TRUST IN LEADERSHIP

Within leadership, trust is the lifeblood that sustains relationships, inspires loyalty, and drives exceptional performance. However, the absence of trust in leadership creates an abyss that engulfs teams and organizations, resulting in profound consequences ripple through every facet of the business. Now, we explore the far-reaching impact of lack of trust in leadership, shedding light on its detrimental effects on individuals, teams, and the overall organizational landscape.

- **Erosion of Employee Morale and Engagement:**

Trust in leadership is necessary to maintain employee morale and engagement. Employees who do not trust their leaders may feel disconnected from the organization's purpose and direction. Disengagement leads to reduced productivity, increased absenteeism, and higher turnover rates as employees become disheartened and seek opportunities elsewhere.

- **Stifled Communication and Collaboration:**

Trust is the foundation of open communication and collaboration within teams. A lack of trust hampers honest dialogue and inhibits the free flow of ideas and feedback. When team members do not trust you, they may withhold information or hesitate to voice their concerns, which impedes effective teamwork and decision-making.

- **Decreased Innovation and Creativity:**

Innovation thrives in an environment of trust, where team members feel safe to take risks and share unconventional ideas. Conversely, lacking trust stifles innovation and creativity, as employees may fear negative consequences for proposing new approaches or challenging the status quo.

- **Low Levels of Employee Loyalty:**

Trust is critical in building employee loyalty and commitment to an organization. When leaders need more trustworthiness, employees may feel more connected to the organization's mission and values. As a result, employees may become more susceptible to external opportunities, leading to lower loyalty and retention levels.

- **Damaged Relationships and Team Dynamics:**

A lack of trust in leadership can fracture relationships within teams and across the organization. Distrust breeds suspicion, leading to a toxic work environment characterized by internal conflicts and interpersonal challenges. As relationships deteriorate, team members' sense of camaraderie and collaboration is severely compromised.

- **Impaired Decision-Making and Risk-Taking:**

Trust is essential for effective decision-making and risk-taking. In an environment lacking trust, team members may second-guess your motives and hesitate to take calculated risks. This caution can lead to missed opportunities and hinder the organization's ability to innovate and adapt to change.

- **Reduced Organizational Resilience:** Organizational resilience relies on trust as a stabilizing force during times of uncertainty. A lack of trust weakens an organization's ability to weather storms and adapt to challenges. As trust erodes, organizational resilience wanes, making it difficult for the company to navigate crises.

- **Negative Impact on Organizational Reputation:** A lack of trust in leadership can severely affect an organization's reputation. When leaders are perceived as untrustworthy, stakeholders, including customers, investors, and partners, may lose faith in the organization's credibility and long-term viability.

- **The decline in Employee Well-Being:**

A lack of trust in leadership can take a toll on employee well-being. Employees who feel disconnected from their leaders and the organization may experience increased stress and a diminished sense of purpose. This decline in well-being can manifest as burnout, anxiety, and reduced job satisfaction.

- **Long-Term Financial Implications:**

Ultimately, a lack of trust in leadership can have long-term financial implications for the organization. Reduced productivity, higher turnover costs, and negative impacts on customer relationships can lead to decreased revenue and profitability over time.

Navigating the abyss of a lack of trust in leadership is a daunting challenge, but it is not insurmountable. By recognizing the far-reaching consequences and understanding trust's critical role in leadership, organizations can take proactive steps to rebuild trust, foster transparency, and prioritize authenticity.

CHAPTER 4

TRUST IN TEAMS AND ORGANIZATIONS: NURTURING A CULTURE OF BELONGING

Trust forms the cornerstone of a thriving culture in the dynamic landscape of teams and organizations. Chapter V explores the vital role of trust in fostering a sense of belonging among team members and within the broader organizational framework. We delve into the transformative power of trust, unraveling how it nurtures collaboration, cohesion, and a shared commitment to success. Join us as we journey to understand how trust cultivates a culture of belonging that empowers teams and you to achieve their fullest potential.

THE TEAM DYNAMIC: TRUST'S INFLUENCE ON COLLABORATION AND PERFORMANCE

In teams, trust is the invisible thread that weaves individuals into a cohesive and high-performing unit. A team that operates on a foundation of trust experiences unparalleled collaboration, productivity, and shared success. Now, we will explore the profound influence of trust on the team dynamic, delving into its transformative impact on collaboration and performance.

- **Psychological Safety: The Bedrock of Trust**

Trust creates a psychological safety net within teams, where members feel comfortable expressing their ideas, opinions, and concerns without fear of judgment or reprisal. In such an environment, team members are likely to take risks, share diverse perspectives, and engage in open discussions, leading to creative problem-solving and innovation.

- **Effective Communication: The Key to Collaborative Success**

Trust is the key to effective communication within teams. When team members trust each other, they are more likely to listen actively, exchange ideas, and provide constructive feedback. This open communication fosters transparency and a deeper understanding of team goals, essential for successful collaboration.

- **Building Cohesion and Unity**

Trust fosters a sense of cohesion and unity among team members. When trust is present, individuals perceive themselves as part of a united front, working collaboratively toward a shared vision. This shared identity creates a strong team culture and reinforces the commitment to achieving common objectives.

- **Conflict Resolution: Navigating Differences with Trust**

In every team, conflicts are inevitable. However, trust enables teams to navigate conflicts constructively and reach resolutions that benefit the entire group. Team members trust that disagreements will be handled respectfully and that diverse viewpoints will be acknowledged and valued.

- **Leveraging Diverse Strengths and Skills**

Trust encourages teams to leverage the diverse strengths and skills of their members. When team members trust each other's expertise and contributions, they are more willing to delegate tasks, seek assistance, and collaborate on projects that align with each individual's expertise.

- **Accountability and Ownership**

A strong sense of accountability and ownership characterizes teams built on trust. Team members take responsibility for their actions and commitments, knowing their colleagues trust them to deliver on their promises. This accountability enhances team performance and fosters a culture of reliability.

- **Flexibility and Adaptability**

Trust empowers teams to be flexible and adaptable in the face of challenges and changes. When team members trust one another, they are more willing to embrace change, take calculated risks, and pivot when necessary. This adaptability is crucial for navigating complex and dynamic work environments.

- **Empowering Innovation and Risk-Taking**

A high level of trust in teams encourages innovation and risk-taking. Team members feel safe exploring new ideas, experimenting, and taking calculated risks without fearing negative consequences. This innovative spirit drives continuous improvement and fosters a culture of learning and growth.

- **Strengthening Commitment and Motivation**

Trust strengthens team members' commitment to shared goals and motivates them to give their best effort. When team members trust their contributions are valued and recognized, they are more engaged and motivated to excel in their roles.

• Sustaining High-Performance Levels

In a trustful team environment, high performance becomes a sustainable norm. Trust nurtures a positive feedback loop, where successful outcomes reinforce trust, leading to greater collaboration, productivity, and performance.

As we explore the influence of trust on the team dynamic, we recognize that trust is not a mere soft factor but a fundamental driver of team success. Teams that prioritize trust cultivate respect, mutual support, and shared purpose.

FORGING AUTHENTIC CONNECTIONS: FOSTERING A CULTURE OF TRUST IN ORGANIZATIONS

In the intricate fabric of organizations, trust serves as the essential thread that binds individuals together, fostering a culture of authenticity, collaboration, and shared purpose. Now, explore the art of forging authentic connections within organizations, unveiling the transformative impact of trust on the workplace culture and its direct influence on employee engagement, loyalty, and organizational success.

- **Trust as the Foundation of Organizational Culture:**

Trust forms the bedrock of a healthy and thriving organizational culture. When trust is woven into the fabric of an organization, employees feel a sense of psychological safety and belonging. This foundation empowers individuals to be themselves, express their ideas, and contribute fully to the organization's mission.

- **Authentic Leadership: Leading by Trustworthy Example:**
Authentic connections in organizations begin with leadership. Authentic leaders prioritize trust, transparency, and open communication. By leading by example and embodying the organization's values, authentic leaders foster a culture of trust that permeates every level of the organization.

- **Encouraging Open Communication and Feedback:**

Organizations that prioritize authentic connections encourage open communication and feedback. Employees feel comfortable expressing their thoughts, concerns, and innovative ideas without fear of retribution. Open dialogue strengthens relationships and empowers employees to shape the organization's direction actively.

- **Building Empathy and Understanding:**

Authentic connections flourish in an environment of empathy and understanding. So, prioritizing empathy fosters a culture of compassion, where employees are attuned to one another's needs and well-being. This empathy leads to stronger bonds among team members and cultivates an atmosphere of mutual support.

- **Transparency and Honesty:**

Transparent communication is a pillar of authentic connections. Organizations that practice transparency build trust by openly sharing information about the organization's goals, challenges, and decisions. This honesty fosters a sense of trustworthiness and credibility within the organization.

- **Embracing Diversity and Inclusion:**

A culture of trust in organizations embraces diversity and inclusion. When employees feel valued and respected for their unique backgrounds and perspectives, they are more likely to bring their authentic selves to work. This inclusivity enriches your organization by leveraging diverse talents and experiences.

- **Recognizing and Valuing Contributions:**

Authentic connections thrive when individuals' contributions are recognized and valued. Organizations that acknowledge and celebrate employees' achievements foster a sense of appreciation and motivation. Recognizing individual and team accomplishments reinforces the culture of trust and inspires continued dedication.

- **Trust-Based Decision-Making:**

Trust-based decision-making empowers employees to contribute to organizational decisions. Organizations that involve employees in decision-making processes foster a sense of ownership and commitment. This participatory approach enhances employees' trust in your organization's leadership.

- **Creating a Learning and Growth Environment:**

Prioritizing authentic connections creates a learning and growth environment. Employees are encouraged to develop new skills, pursue professional development, and take on challenging assignments. This investment in employees' growth reinforces their trust in your commitment to their well-being and success.

- **Resolving Conflicts with Respect:**

In organizations with authentic connections, conflicts are addressed with respect and a focus on resolution. Employees trust that conflicts will be handled constructively and without favoritism. This approach fosters a culture of fairness and unity.

As we explore the art of forging authentic connections in organizations, we recognize that trust is the catalyst that ignites employee engagement, fosters collaboration, and fuels organizational success. Organizations that prioritize trust cultivate a culture where employees feel valued, empowered, and inspired to achieve greatness.

BREAKING BARRIERS: OVERCOMING TRUST CHALLENGES IN THE WORKPLACE

Trust is the lifeblood of healthy and productive workplaces. However, in the complex and dynamic world of work, various challenges can impede the cultivation of trust among employees and within teams. Chapter V explores the diverse barriers to trust in the workplace and delves into effective strategies for overcoming these obstacles, fostering a culture of trust, and cultivating a thriving and cohesive work environment.

- **Lack of Communication:**

A significant barrier to trust in the workplace is the need for open and effective communication. When employees and teams do not communicate transparently, misunderstandings and misinterpretations can arise, eroding trust among colleagues. Overcoming this challenge requires promoting a culture of open dialogue, active listening, and honest feedback.

- **Fear of Vulnerability:**

Many employees hesitate to be vulnerable at work due to concerns about judgment or reprisal. However, vulnerability is essential for building trust and authentic connections. You will overcome this barrier by demonstrating vulnerability and creating a safe space where employees feel comfortable expressing their thoughts and emotions.

- **Past Breaches of Trust:**

Past breaches of trust, whether real or perceived, can create lasting barriers in the workplace; to overcome this challenge, organizations must address historical issues transparently, apologize when necessary, and take concrete steps to rebuild trust. Consistent and trustworthy behavior over time will help repair fractured relationships.

- **Lack of Empathy:**

Empathy is a fundamental element of trust in the workplace. Trust can suffer when employees feel that their colleagues or you lack empathy. To break this barrier, you must prioritize empathy training, foster a culture of compassion, and encourage understanding of each other's perspectives and feelings.

- **Micromanagement:**

Micromanagement can be a significant hindrance to trust and employee empowerment. Employees who feel their work is constantly scrutinized may need to be more motivated and engaged. You will overcome this barrier by delegating tasks, providing autonomy, and trusting employees to fulfill their responsibilities.

- **Lack of Clear Goals and Expectations:**

Clear goals and expectations can lead to clarity and trust in the workplace. Employees may feel uncertain about what is expected of them, leading to a breakdown in trust. Overcoming this challenge requires setting clear and realistic goals, providing clear guidelines, and ensuring that employees understand their roles and responsibilities.

- **Office Politics and Favoritism:**

Office politics and favoritism can erode employee trust and create a sense of unfairness in the workplace. You must address this barrier by promoting a culture of fairness and transparency, rewarding performance based on merit, and fostering an inclusive environment where all employees are valued.

- **Lack of Recognition and Appreciation:**

Trust can wane when employees feel they need to be recognized or appreciated for their efforts. You should prioritize recognition and appreciation as essential components of your culture to overcome this challenge. Celebrating achievements and expressing gratitude for hard work strengthens trust and boosts employee morale.

- **Resistance to Change:**

Resistance to change can create barriers to trust, as employees may feel anxious about uncertain outcomes. Leaders can overcome this challenge by involving employees in the change process, providing clear communication about the reasons for change, and emphasizing the organization's commitment to supporting employees through transitions.

- **Unresolved Conflicts:**

Unresolved conflicts can fester and create a toxic work environment, damaging employee trust.

Leaders should address conflicts promptly, encourage open dialogue, and mediate when necessary to promote resolution. Transparent conflict resolution builds trust and fosters a culture of respect.

By proactively addressing these barriers to trust, organizations can create a workplace culture where trust thrives, relationships flourish, and employees feel empowered to bring their authentic selves to work.

CHAPTER 5

TRUST IN COMMUNICATION AND TRANSPARENCY: BUILDING BRIDGES OF OPENNESS

Now, we will explore the pivotal role of trust in communication and transparency—a dynamic duo that bridges gaps, fosters understanding, and strengthens relationships. In this chapter, we delve into the power of open and honest communication, uncovering how transparency creates an environment of trust that empowers individuals and organizations to thrive. Join us as we embark on a journey of authentic dialogue, unraveling the transformative impact of building bridges through openness and trust.

TRANSPARENT TRUTHS: THE POWER OF CLEAR COMMUNICATION IN RESTORING TRUST

Clear and transparent communication serves as a beacon of trust, illuminating the path to understanding, resolution, and reconciliation. Now, we will explore the profound impact of transparent truths on restoring trust in organizations, and communities.

- **The Healing Power of Transparent Communication:**

Transparent communication is a healing balm that soothes wounds and restores trust. Honesty and openness in a business organization:

1. Create a safe space for individuals to express feelings, concerns, and vulnerabilities.

2. Foster an environment where trust can take root and flourish.

3. Encourage open communication, collaboration, and idea-sharing.

4. Build strong working relationships and increase employee engagement.

5. Nurtures a culture that empowers individuals and drives organizational success.

- **Acknowledging Past Mistakes: The Path to Forgiveness:**

Transparent truths require acknowledging past mistakes and taking responsibility for one's actions. How embracing accountability paves the way for forgiveness and rebuilding trust:

1. Acknowledge past missteps.

2. Demonstrate genuine remorse.

3. Commit to change.

4. Transparency and honesty.

5. Consistent actions.

6. Patience and understanding.

7. Open communication.

8. Setting boundaries.

9. Cultivate empathy.

10. Learning from the past.

11. Consistent effort.

12. Forgiveness as a choice.

- **The Language of Honesty: Fostering Authenticity:**

Honesty becomes the language of trust as individuals express their authentic thoughts and emotions. Embracing authenticity in communication:

1. Fosters deeper understanding.

2. Strengthens bonds within relationships.

3. Strengthens bonds within communities.

- **Repairing Broken Trust through Communication:**

When trust is broken, communication becomes the bridge to repair the damage. Open dialogue and sincere apologies in restoring trust:

1. Open dialogue promotes honest communication.

2. Sincere apologies acknowledge wrongdoing.

3. Both are essential in rebuilding trust.

4. Create a safe space for understanding.

5. Foster accountability and responsibility.

6. Encourage empathy and compassion.

7. Facilitate healing and reconciliation.

8. Strengthen bonds within relationships.

9. Rebuild trust in organizations.

10. Demonstrate commitment to positive change.

- **The Power of Clarity in Communication:**

Clarity in communication is paramount to avoid misunderstandings and misinterpretations. Clear and transparent messaging fosters trust by ensuring everyone is on the same page:

1. Eliminates confusion and misunderstandings.
2. Builds confidence in leadership and decision-making.
3. Demonstrates honesty and integrity in communication.
4. Encourages open dialogue and feedback.
5. Reduces rumors and speculation.
6. Promotes a culture of accountability and responsibility.
7. Empowers individuals to make informed decisions.
8. Strengthens team alignment and collaboration.
9. Enhances overall organizational transparency.
10. Builds trust by valuing open and honest communication.

- **Embracing Difficult Conversations:**

Transparent communication includes navigating difficult conversations with grace and respect. Addressing sensitive topics openly in relationships and teams:

1. Promotes honesty and transparency.
2. Creates a safe space for open communication.
3. Encourages mutual understanding and empathy.
4. Fosters trust through vulnerability and authenticity.
5. Prevents misunderstandings and assumptions.
6. Builds a culture of trust and respect.

7. Strengthens team cohesion and collaboration.

8. Demonstrates a commitment to addressing challenges.

9. Empowers individuals to share their perspectives.

10. Drives meaningful problem-solving and growth.

- **Navigating Trust in a Digital Age:**

In a digital world, transparent communication faces new challenges. Importance of navigating trust in online interactions:

1. Safeguarding privacy builds user confidence.

2. Clear communication fosters understanding and prevents misunderstandings.

3. Transparent policies and practices establish credibility.

4. Addressing privacy concerns nurtures trust in digital platforms.

5. Building trust ensures long-term customer loyalty.

6. Trustworthy interactions enhance brand reputation.

7. Trust is the foundation for successful online relationships and transactions.

UNRAVELING DECEPTION: ADDRESSING RUMORS, MISINFORMATION, AND CORPORATE SECRECY

Deception, in its many forms, casts a shadow on trust and creates barriers to genuine connections.

- **The Deceptive Web: Understanding the Impact of Rumors:**

Rumors weave a deceptive web that spreads like wildfire, eroding trust and sowing discord. We'll explore how rumors take root, the psychological impact they have on individuals and communities, and strategies for dispelling misinformation.

1. Rumors take root through incomplete information and speculation.

2. Psychological impact includes anxiety, fear, and mistrust in individuals and communities.

3. Rumors can lead to social division and damage relationships.

4. Strategies for dispelling misinformation include proactive communication.

5. Providing accurate and timely information helps combat rumors.

6. Encouraging critical thinking and media literacy reduces the spread of false information.

7. Building trust in reliable sources and fact-checking ensures a more informed society.

- **Unraveling Deception in the Digital Age:**

In the fast-paced and interconnected world of the digital age, deception lurks in the shadows, presenting significant challenges to trust-building. As you, the leader, navigate the intricate web of trust in the digital landscape, it becomes crucial to comprehend the multifaceted nature of deception, its detrimental impact on individuals and organizations, and the strategies to counteract it.

1. The Digital Frontier of Deception: The digital age has brought forth new frontiers for deception, including online scams, phishing emails, fake news, and deep fake videos. Understand the various forms of deception that can undermine trust in the digital realm.

2. Psychological Impact of Deception: Deception can have profound psychological effects on individuals. Explore how falling victim to deception can erode trust, induce feelings of vulnerability, and foster skepticism in the digital realm.

3. Building Digital Resilience: Empower yourself and your organization with digital resilience to counteract deception. Develop a culture of critical thinking and digital literacy, enabling individuals to identify and question deceptive content.

4. Transparency and Authenticity: Emphasize transparency and authenticity in your digital communications. Foster an environment where genuine and trustworthy content prevails, ensuring that your digital footprint reflects honesty and integrity.

5. Combating Fake News: In the era of misinformation, equip yourself with the tools to combat fake news. Encourage fact-checking and rely on credible sources to disseminate accurate information, contributing to a more trustworthy digital ecosystem.

6. Cybersecurity and Data Protection: Trust in the digital age is deeply intertwined with cybersecurity and data protection. Implement robust security measures to safeguard sensitive data, protecting your organization and customers from potential deception.

7. Vigilance against Phishing and Scams: Educate your team on the dangers of phishing and online scams. Empower them to recognize suspicious communications and report potential threats promptly.

8. Verifying Online Identities: In the digital landscape, verifying online identities is paramount. Establish procedures to verify the authenticity of digital profiles and accounts, reducing the risk of deception by imposters.

9. Addressing Deep fake Challenges: With the rise of deepfake technology, the potential for deception grows exponentially. Explore strategies to address deepfake challenges, such as watermarking or digital signature verification.

10. Ethics in Digital Communications: Uphold ethical standards in your digital communications. Embrace responsible content creation and distribution, avoiding deceptive tactics that erode trust with your audience.

11. Fostering Digital Trustworthiness: Nurture digital trustworthiness across your organization. Train employees to be trustworthy digital ambassadors, as their actions and interactions can significantly impact your organization's reputation.

12. Strengthening Online Reputation: Your online reputation is a valuable asset. Prioritize building a positive and authentic online presence, fostering trust with your audience and stakeholders.

13. Addressing Trolls and Cyberbullying: Deception can manifest in the form of online harassment and cyberbullying. Take a strong stance against such behavior, fostering a safe digital space for your employees, customers, and community.

14. Embracing Transparent Communication: Emphasize transparent communication in your digital interactions. Address concerns openly and honestly, building credibility and trust in your online engagements.

15. Digital Crisis Management: Prepare for potential digital crises by developing a robust crisis management plan. Respond promptly and transparently to digital challenges, showcasing your commitment to honesty and trust.

16. Emphasizing Privacy and Consent: Respect privacy and consent in your digital interactions. Obtain explicit consent before collecting and using personal data, reassuring your audience that their information is secure.

17. Building Trust in Online Transactions: For businesses, building trust in online transactions is vital. Implement secure payment gateways and display trust symbols to instill confidence in your customers.

18. Encouraging Digital Citizenship: Promote digital citizenship within your organization and community. Encourage responsible online behavior, nurturing a digital culture founded on trust and respect.

19. Leveraging Digital Trust Seals: Display digital trust seals from reputable organizations to validate your credibility and commitment to cybersecurity.

20. Continuous Learning and Adaptation: The digital landscape is ever-evolving. Embrace continuous learning and adaptability to stay ahead of deceptive tactics and maintain trust in the digital age.

In conclusion, the digital age presents both opportunities and challenges for trust-building. As you navigate the complex landscape of deception, your vigilance, transparency, and commitment to authentic communication will be the pillars of a trustworthy digital presence. Embrace your role as a digital leader, empowering your organization to foster a culture of digital trustworthiness, dispelling deception, and ensuring that your digital footprint reflects the honesty and integrity needed to thrive in the digital era.

- **Trustworthy Leadership: Leading with Integrity:**

Trustworthy leadership sets the tone for transparency and accountability within organizations. We'll discuss the qualities of trustworthy leaders, including integrity, authenticity, and a commitment to open communication. Let's delve deeper into each of these qualities:

1. Integrity:

Integrity is the cornerstone of trustworthy leadership. Leaders with integrity consistently act in alignment with their values, principles, and ethical standards. They are honest, transparent, and uphold a strong sense of moral character. Employees trust leaders who demonstrate unwavering integrity because they know that these leaders will make decisions based on what is right, not what is expedient or self-serving. Integrity also involves taking responsibility for one's actions, admitting mistakes, and learning from them, which further strengthens trust and credibility.

2. Authenticity:

Authentic leaders are genuine and true to themselves. They don't wear a mask or project a false image; instead, they embrace their strengths and vulnerabilities openly. This genuine approach fosters a sense of connection and relatability with their teams. When leaders are authentic, employees feel more comfortable expressing their ideas, concerns, and feedback. Authentic leaders create an environment where employees feel seen, heard, and valued, which enhances trust and psychological safety within the organization.

3. Commitment to Open Communication:

Effective leaders prioritize open and transparent communication. They understand the importance of keeping employees informed about the organization's goals, strategies, challenges, and successes. Trustworthy leaders actively seek feedback from their teams and encourage open dialogue. They create channels for employees to voice their opinions and concerns without fear of retribution. Transparent communication builds trust by reducing uncertainty and fostering a culture of accountability and mutual respect.

4. Consistency:

Trustworthy leaders are consistent in their actions and decision-making. They don't waver in their values or behaviors, even in challenging situations. Employees can rely on consistent leaders to make fair and just decisions, which reinforces the belief that their leader has their best interests at heart. Consistency also helps build a sense of stability and predictability within the organization, reducing anxiety and increasing confidence in leadership.

5. Empathy and Emotional Intelligence:

Leaders who demonstrate empathy and emotional intelligence understand the emotions and perspectives of their team members. They actively listen, show empathy, and consider the feelings and needs of others. Empathetic leaders create a supportive and caring environment, where employees feel valued as individuals. By understanding the human aspect of their workforce, these leaders build stronger connections and trust with their teams.

6. Competence and Expertise:

Trustworthy leaders are knowledgeable and competent in their roles. They have the skills and expertise required to lead effectively and make informed decisions. Employees trust leaders who can confidently guide the organization towards success and provide direction based on their expertise. Demonstrating competence builds trust in a leader's ability to navigate challenges and create a vision for the future.

In summary, trustworthy leaders embody qualities such as integrity, authenticity, and a commitment to open communication. By being true to yourself, maintaining ethical standards, and fostering an environment of openness and empathy, you will inspire trust and loyalty within your teams. Your consistency, competence, and genuine care for your employees create a strong foundation for a positive and productive work culture. Trustworthy leadership is not only essential for building strong teams but also for driving long-term organizational success and growth.

THE HEART OF DIALOGUE: CREATING OPEN CHANNELS FOR TRUST-BUILDING

In the realm of leadership, effective communication is the cornerstone of building and maintaining trust within teams and organizations. As you, the leader, embark on the journey of fostering a culture of trust, it is essential to understand the significance of open dialogue and its profound impact on trust-building. This comprehensive exploration delves into the heart of dialogue, uncovering the power it holds in nurturing trust, enhancing collaboration, and creating a cohesive and resilient workforce.

1. Understanding the Essence of Dialogue: Dialogue goes beyond mere conversation; it is a purposeful exchange of ideas, thoughts, and emotions. Embrace the art of active listening and empathetic understanding, laying the groundwork for open and honest conversations.

2. Laying the Foundation of Trust: Trust and dialogue share a symbiotic relationship. Explore how trust is fortified through open channels of communication, as authentic dialogue cultivates a safe space where individuals feel valued, heard, and respected.

3. Vulnerability and Connection: The heart of dialogue thrives on vulnerability. Encourage and model vulnerability within your organization, as it fosters authentic connections and empowers individuals to share their thoughts and concerns openly.

4. Bridging the Gap in Hierarchies: Hierarchies can sometimes hinder open dialogue. Break down barriers by creating a culture where everyone feels comfortable sharing their perspectives, regardless of their position in the organization.

5. The Power of Inclusivity: Inclusive dialogue welcomes diverse voices and perspectives. Embrace inclusivity within your teams, appreciating the richness it brings to discussions and the trust it instills in all members.

6. Building Psychological Safety: Psychological safety is the bedrock of trust-building dialogue. Nurture an environment where individuals feel psychologically secure, enabling them to speak up without fear of judgment or reprisal.

7. Embracing Difficult Conversations: Addressing sensitive topics can be challenging but essential. Equip yourself with the skills to navigate difficult conversations with empathy and tact, fostering understanding and resolution.

8. Active Listening as a Superpower: Listening attentively is a leadership superpower. Cultivate active listening skills, valuing the thoughts and concerns of others, and demonstrating your commitment to their well-being.

9. Empowering Through Feedback: Constructive feedback is a vital component of dialogue. Deliver feedback with care, focusing on growth and improvement, and showcasing your dedication to individual and collective success.

10. Recognizing Non-Verbal Cues: Communication transcends words. Pay attention to non-verbal cues, as they reveal underlying emotions and allow you to respond with empathy and understanding.

11. The Role of Authenticity: Authenticity breathes life into dialogue. Be genuine in your interactions, as authenticity builds trust and strengthens the emotional connections between leaders and their teams.

12. Cultivating Curiosity: Curiosity is the fuel that drives meaningful dialogue. Encourage curiosity within your organization, as it ignites a thirst for learning and discovery, leading to innovative solutions and strengthened trust.

13. Resolving Conflict Through Dialogue: Conflict is an inevitable part of human interaction. Embrace conflict as an opportunity for growth, engaging in constructive dialogue to address disagreements and reach resolutions that strengthen relationships.

14. Dialogue as a Tool for Collaboration: Collaboration thrives in a culture of open dialogue. Harness the power of dialogue to facilitate collaboration, uniting team members in a shared vision and purpose.

15. Leveraging Technology for Dialogue: In the digital age, technology plays a pivotal role in facilitating dialogue. Embrace technological tools that enable seamless communication and collaboration, promoting trust within virtual and remote teams.

16. Celebrating Success and Progress: Dialogue extends beyond problem-solving; it also celebrates success and progress. Acknowledge achievements openly, reinforcing a culture of appreciation and motivating individuals to strive for excellence.

17. Sustaining Dialogue through Change: In times of change, dialogue becomes even more critical. Sustain open channels of communication during transitions, reassuring your teams and preserving trust amid uncertainty.

18. Leading by Example: As a leader, your actions set the tone for dialogue within your organization. Lead by example, demonstrating a commitment to open communication and trust-building in all aspects of your leadership.

19. Encouraging Dialogue Across Departments: Break down silos by encouraging dialogue across departments and teams. Facilitate cross-functional discussions to foster collaboration, share insights, and build a cohesive organizational culture.

20. Nurturing a Learning Culture: Dialogue and learning are intertwined. Cultivate a learning culture that encourages curiosity, feedback, and open dialogue, empowering individuals and teams to embrace growth and continuous improvement.

In conclusion, the heart of dialogue forms the bedrock of trust-building within your organization. By embracing open channels of communication, actively listening to your team members, and nurturing an inclusive and learning-oriented culture, you can create an environment where trust thrives, relationships flourish, and your organization achieves greater heights of success. Empower yourself with the profound influence of dialogue and seize the opportunity to foster a cohesive, resilient, and high-performing workforce, firmly anchored in trust.

Chapter 6

The Pyramid Trust in Action: Empowering Positive Change

As you, the leader, delve into the depths of trust's transformative power, it becomes evident that trust is not merely an abstract concept but a catalyst for positive change in individuals, relationships, organizations, and society at large. The Pyramid Trust is an awe-inspiring phenomenon that reverberates far beyond its initial impact, creating a web of interconnected transformation that spreads like ripples in a pond. This comprehensive exploration takes you on a profound journey through inspiring insights, and actionable strategies that exemplify The Pyramid Trust in action.

1. Trust as a Catalyst for Positive Change: Trust sets in motion a series of transformative actions that influence every aspect of our lives. Explore the concept of The Pyramid Trust, on understanding how a single act of trust can spark a chain reaction of positive change.

2. Unleashing the Potential of Individuals: Trust empowers individuals to reach their full potential. As a leader, foster an environment where individuals feel secure in expressing their ideas and taking calculated risks, unleashing their creative and innovative capabilities.

3. Building Resilient Relationships: Trust is the cornerstone of resilient relationships. Dive into the power of trust in forging bonds, resolving conflicts, and weathering challenges together, fostering deeper connections among team members.

4. The Impact on Organizational Culture: Trust shapes the very fabric of organizational culture. Examine how a culture of trust cultivates employee engagement, loyalty, and a sense of belonging, leading to improved productivity and overall performance.

5. Trust's Amplifying Effect on Leadership: As a leader, your trust in your team members amplifies their sense of responsibility and commitment. Understand how your trust in others can fuel their confidence and drive for success.

6. Trusting Across Organizational Levels: Trust is not limited to top-down relationships. Explore the significance of horizontal trust among team members, as well as trust between leaders and subordinates, in creating a cohesive and high-functioning organization.

7. The Role of Transparency and Communication: Transparent communication is the lifeblood of The Pyramid Trust. Embrace open and honest communication, fostering an environment where information flows freely and trust flourishes.

8. Trust and Conflict Resolution: Conflict is inevitable, but trust can lead to effective resolution. Learn how trust-based dialogue and empathy can transform conflicts into opportunities for growth and understanding.

9. Trust in Crisis Management: During times of crisis, trust becomes even more critical. Discover how trust in leadership and decision-making can help organizations navigate challenging situations and emerge stronger.

10. Trust's Impact on Decision-Making: Trust influences decision-making processes. Explore how a culture of trust encourages shared decision-making, where diverse perspectives are valued and collective wisdom drives better outcomes.

11. The Pyramid Trust in Customer Relationships: Trust is the cornerstone of customer loyalty. Analyze how trust builds lasting relationships with customers, fostering brand loyalty and advocacy.

12. The Pyramid Trust in Supply Chain and Partnerships: Trust extends beyond organizational boundaries. Examine how The Pyramid Trust influences supply chain relationships, collaborations, and partnerships, creating a robust and interdependent ecosystem.

13. Pyramid Trust in Society: Trust is a force that transcends organizational boundaries. Delve into stories of real-life champions who have catalyzed positive change in society through trust, leaving a lasting legacy for generations to come.

14. Sustaining The Pyramid Trust: Trust requires continuous nurturing. Uncover strategies to sustain The Pyramid Trust, ensuring that its transformative power endures and flourishes over time.

15. Inspiring a Pyramid Trust Effect Beyond Yourself: As you experience the profound impact of trust in action, inspire others to embrace The Pyramid Trust in their own lives and leadership journeys, creating a collective wave of positive change.

In conclusion, The Pyramid Trust is a testament to the boundless potential of trust as a force for positive change. As you harness the power of trust in your leadership, relationships, and organizational culture, you become an integral part of a transformative ripple that extends far beyond your immediate sphere of influence. Embrace The Pyramid Trust in action, empowering yourself and others to create a world where trust becomes the catalyst for empowerment, growth, and lasting transformation. As you embrace this journey, you will witness the remarkable impact of trust on individuals, organizations, and society, leaving a trail of positive change that enriches lives and shapes a better future for all.

A. THE INTERCONNECTED WEB: TRUST'S ROLE IN TRANSFORMING INDIVIDUALS AND RELATIONSHIPS

Trust weaves an interconnected web that transcends individual interactions, shaping the landscape of relationships and transforming lives. This chapter delves into the profound role of trust in empowering positive change at the individual and relational levels. From building self-confidence to nurturing vulnerability, we'll explore how trust is the cornerstone for personal growth and flourishing connections.

The Interconnected Web: Trust's Role in Transforming Individuals and Relationships

As you, the leader, embark on a profound exploration of trust's transformative power, you will uncover the intricate and far-reaching nature of the interconnected web that trust weaves. Trust is not just a singular thread that binds individuals and relationships; it forms a tapestry of connections that reverberate across every facet of our lives. In this comprehensive and extensive discussion, we will delve into the profound impact of trust as it navigates the complex pathways of our thoughts, emotions, and actions, ultimately leading to profound transformations in individuals and relationships.

1. Understanding the Fabric of Trust: Trust forms the very fabric of human connections. As you analyze the threads of trust that intertwine, you will begin to comprehend how trust influences your beliefs, perceptions, and interactions with others.

2. Trust's Role in Emotional Resonance: Trust resonates deeply within us, impacting our emotional well-being and fostering a sense of security in our relationships. Explore how trust acts as a powerful force in cultivating emotional connections, enabling individuals to share vulnerabilities and experiences without fear.

3. The Pyramid Trust in Relationships: Trust initiates a pyramid effect in relationships, building a sense of reciprocity, empathy, and understanding. You will uncover how trust enhances communication, fosters authenticity, and nurtures a safe space for vulnerability and growth.

4. Building Bridges of Empathy: Trust paves the way for empathy, allowing individuals to step into one another's shoes and perceive the world from a different perspective. Embrace the profound role of trust in fostering compassion and genuine connections.

5. Trust's Impact on Decision-Making: As you navigate the interconnected web of trust, you will realize how trust affects the decision-making process. Trust encourages collaboration, leading to better-informed choices and collective ownership of outcomes.

6. The Unwavering Connection between Trust and Integrity: Trust and integrity are inseparable companions. Dive into the correlation between trust and integrity, understanding how integrity serves as the foundation for establishing and nurturing trust in individuals and relationships.

7. Trust as a Catalyst for Personal Growth: Trust acts as a catalyst for personal growth, empowering individuals to embrace challenges, take calculated risks, and expand their horizons. As you build trust within yourself, you cultivate the resilience needed to face life's uncertainties.

8. Vulnerability: The Key to Unlocking Trust's Potential: Embrace vulnerability as a conduit for trust. Discover how embracing vulnerability allows individuals to foster deeper connections, break down barriers, and invite others to reciprocate trust.

9. Trust's Impact on Organizational Culture:
Trust cascades through the interconnected web, influencing organizational culture at its core. You will explore how a culture of trust within teams and organizations cultivates collaboration, innovation, and a shared sense of purpose.

10. Navigating the Interconnected Web in Times of Crisis: In times of crisis, trust becomes an anchor that steadies the ship. Examine how trust in leadership and transparent communication can help individuals and organizations navigate the stormy waters of uncertainty.

11. The Paradox of Trust and Risk: Trust involves an element of risk, as individuals invest their faith in others. Delve into the delicate balance between trust and risk, understanding how calculated trust can lead to profound rewards.

12. Trust's Influence on Conflict Resolution: As you unravel the interconnected web of trust, you will recognize its instrumental role in conflict resolution. Trust fosters open dialogue, allowing for respectful disagreements and collaborative problem-solving.

13. The Butterfly Effect of Trust: Trust's impact goes beyond its immediate connections. Explore how the butterfly effect of trust influences communities, industries, and society at large, transforming the world one relationship at a time.

14. Embracing Trust's Legacy: Trust leaves a lasting legacy that transcends time. Reflect on the significance of trust's enduring impact on individuals and relationships, influencing future generations and shaping a better world.

15. Empowering Transformation Through Trust: As you navigate the interconnected web of trust, you will witness its potential to empower profound transformation. Embrace trust as the cornerstone of personal growth, nurturing authentic relationships, and fostering a world where the power of trust creates lasting impact.

In conclusion, the interconnected web of trust is a complex and awe-inspiring tapestry that shapes the course of our lives and relationships. As you, the leader, unravel its intricate patterns, you will gain a deeper appreciation for the transformative power of trust in individual growth and relationship dynamics. Embrace the role of trust as a catalyst for empathy, authenticity, and collective growth, as it weaves an interconnected web that elevates individuals, strengthens relationships, and ultimately transforms our world. Trust's enduring legacy lies in your hands, empowering you to create a pyramid trust of positive change through the transformative power of trust.

CHAPTER 7

OVERCOMING TRUST BARRIERS: BREAKING FREE FROM DOUBT AND DISTRUST

In this chapter, we confront the intricate challenges that hinder trust's transformative potential. Doubt and distrust cast shadows on the trust-building path, creating barriers that impede meaningful connections and positive change.

Understanding the roots of doubt and distrust empowers us to embrace vulnerability, rebuild shattered trust, and cultivate a trustful space where individuals and communities can flourish.

THE BARRIER DISCOVERY: IDENTIFYING COMMON OBSTACLES TO TRUST AND TRANSFORMATION

In the pursuit of trust and transformation, individuals, teams, and organizations must navigate through a myriad of barriers that can hinder progress. The process of Barrier Discovery is crucial as it sheds light on the challenges that inhibit the development of trust and the realization of transformative goals. By comprehensively understanding and addressing these obstacles, we can lay the foundation for building enduring and meaningful relationships that foster positive change.

By identifying and understanding these obstacles, we equip ourselves with the tools needed to navigate through doubt and distrust, paving the way for meaningful connections and positive change.

1. Fear of Vulnerability: At the heart of many trust barriers lies the fear of vulnerability. One of the most common barriers to trust is the fear of vulnerability. Opening oneself up to others, sharing emotions, thoughts, and weaknesses, requires courage. However, the fear of being judged, betrayed, or taken advantage of can deter individuals from being authentic and genuine in their interactions.

This fear hampers the formation of deep connections and creates a surface-level rapport that lacks the necessary trust for transformation to occur.

2. Past Betrayals and Breaches: Experiences of betrayal or breaches of trust in the past can leave deep emotional scars that influence future relationships. When individuals have been let down or deceived by others, they become cautious and guarded, hesitant to trust again. These wounds from the past can taint new interactions, making it challenging to forge meaningful connections and hindering progress in any transformational journey.

3. Communication Barriers: Effective communication is at the core of building trust. Miscommunication, lack of transparency, and unclear intentions can lead to misunderstandings and create mistrust. When messages are misinterpreted, assumptions are made, and intentions are questioned, the trust-building process falters. Addressing communication barriers is essential to establishing clarity, fostering open dialogue, and ensuring that all parties involved are on the same page.

4. Power Imbalance: In the context of organizations, power imbalances between leaders and employees can create a sense of mistrust within the workforce. When individuals feel unheard, undervalued, or disregarded by those in positions of authority, it undermines trust in leadership and impacts overall team dynamics. Trust flourishes when individuals feel valued and empowered, regardless of their hierarchical position.

5. Lack of Accountability: Accountability is a fundamental element of trust-building. When individuals fail to take responsibility for their actions and decisions, it erodes trust in relationships and organizations. A lack of accountability fosters a culture of blame and evades ownership, making it difficult to move forward and achieve transformational goals.

6. Cultural and Diversity Differences: Diverse perspectives and cultural backgrounds enrich relationships and teams. However, if not properly understood and respected, these differences can lead to misunderstandings and miscommunication. Embracing diversity and learning to navigate cultural differences is essential to fostering a culture of inclusion and trust.

7. Inconsistent Behavior: Consistency in actions and words is vital for building trust. When individuals exhibit inconsistent behavior or fail to follow through on commitments, it can lead to doubt and uncertainty about their intentions and reliability. Trust is built on the foundation of reliability and consistency.

8. Perception of Hidden Agendas: Trust can be hindered when individuals perceive hidden agendas in others' actions. When motives are perceived as self-serving or deceptive, suspicion and doubt arise, making it difficult to establish a sense of trust. Transparent and open communication is crucial to dispelling any perceptions of hidden motives and fostering a culture of honesty.

9. Resistance to Change: During times of transformation and change, individuals may resist embracing new ideas or approaches. Fear of the unknown or concerns about potential negative consequences can hinder trust in the process. Addressing resistance to change requires effective communication, providing support, and demonstrating the benefits of transformation to build trust and gain commitment from all stakeholders.

10. Lack of Emotional Intelligence: Emotional intelligence plays a vital role in building trust. Individuals with high emotional intelligence can understand and empathize with others' emotions, facilitating deeper connections. On the other hand, a lack of emotional intelligence may result in misunderstandings, misinterpretations, and an inability to effectively navigate emotionally charged situations.

Strategies for Overcoming Barriers

1. Foster Psychological Safety: Create an environment where individuals feel safe to be vulnerable, express themselves openly, and share their feelings without fear of judgment or retribution. Encourage a culture of respect and empathy, where opinions and concerns are valued.

2. Learn from Past Experiences: Address past betrayals and breaches openly, acknowledge the pain and emotional impact, and work towards healing and rebuilding trust. Engage in honest conversations to gain insight into what went wrong and how trust can be rebuilt.

3. Promote Transparent and Open Communication: Encourage clear and honest communication to minimize misunderstandings and build trust through openness. Provide regular opportunities for feedback, active listening, and open dialogue.

4. Empower Employees: Ensure that everyone's voice is heard, regardless of their position, to reduce power imbalances and foster a sense of belonging. Encourage participatory decision-making to build trust in organizational leadership.

5. Encourage Accountability: Hold individuals accountable for their actions and decisions, promoting a culture of responsibility and trust. Encourage a mindset of taking ownership of one's mistakes and learning from them.

6. Embrace Diversity and Inclusion: Celebrate diverse perspectives and cultural backgrounds, creating an inclusive environment that values differences and fosters mutual understanding.

7. Consistency in Actions: Demonstrate consistency in behavior, aligning words with actions, to build trust through reliability. Deliver on commitments consistently and follow through on promises.

8. Transparency in Intentions: Be open about goals and intentions, dispelling any perceptions of hidden agendas. Communicate openly about decisions, strategies, and future plans to build trust through transparency.

9. Manage Change Effectively: Communicate the benefits of transformation, address concerns, and provide support to alleviate resistance to change. Involve stakeholders in the process and provide clear guidance on navigating the changes.

10. Develop Emotional Intelligence: Invest in emotional intelligence training to enhance understanding and empathy, strengthening interpersonal connections and building trust through emotional awareness.

Identifying and addressing these common obstacles to trust and transformation lays the groundwork for building resilient relationships and thriving organizations. By embracing these strategies, individuals and teams can create a culture of trust, empowerment, and growth, leading to profound and sustainable transformations that positively impact personal and professional lives.

- **Emotional Baggage: Carrying Old Burdens**

Emotional baggage from past experiences can weigh us down, impacting our ability to trust and embrace transformation. We'll explore how addressing and processing emotional baggage is crucial for breaking free from trust barriers.

Addressing and processing emotional baggage is a crucial step in breaking free from trust barriers and fostering a positive and productive work environment. As a business leader, you must recognize that emotional baggage significantly impacts your ability to build trust and establish meaningful connections with your team.

Strategies to help you address and process emotional baggage effectively:

1. Self-Reflection and Awareness:

Start by engaging in self-reflection and developing self-awareness. Take the time to understand your own emotions, triggers, and past experiences that might be influencing your interactions with others. Acknowledge any emotional baggage you may carry and be honest with yourself about its potential impact on your leadership style.

2. Seek Support and Feedback:

Don't hesitate to seek support from a trusted colleague, mentor, or even a professional coach or therapist. Talking openly about your emotional challenges and seeking constructive feedback can provide valuable insights and guidance on how to address and process your emotional baggage effectively.

3. Practice Emotional Intelligence:

Emotional intelligence is essential for managing emotions and building trust. Develop your emotional intelligence by actively listening to your team members, empathizing with their experiences, and validating their emotions. Avoid reacting impulsively and instead, respond to situations with empathy and understanding.

4. Embrace Vulnerability:

Show vulnerability and authenticity in your leadership approach. Admitting that you may have emotional baggage can create a safe space for others to share their feelings and concerns as well. Leading by example and being open about your own growth journey encourages others to do the same, fostering a culture of trust and support.

5. Provide Psychological Safety:

Create a work environment that promotes psychological safety, where team members feel comfortable expressing their thoughts and emotions without fear of judgment or repercussions. Encourage open communication, active listening, and constructive feedback.

6. Encourage Team-Building Activities:

Organize team-building activities that encourage bonding and trust among team members. Engaging in shared experiences outside of work can help break down barriers and build stronger connections within the team.

7. Set Clear Expectations:

Establish clear expectations for behavior and communication within the team. Reinforce the importance of trust and open dialogue, and address any behavior that undermines trust promptly and constructively.

8. Invest in Training and Development:

Consider investing in emotional intelligence and communication training for yourself and your team. Equipping your team with the tools and skills to navigate emotions and conflicts effectively will strengthen trust and collaboration.

9. Foster a Culture of Forgiveness:

Recognize that addressing emotional baggage involves forgiveness, both towards yourself and others. Encourage a culture of forgiveness and second chances, where mistakes are viewed as opportunities for growth and learning.

10. Monitor Progress and Celebrate Success:

Regularly monitor your progress in addressing and processing emotional baggage. Celebrate the positive changes and improvements in trust and team dynamics. Recognize the efforts of team members who contribute to a trusting and supportive work environment.

Breaking free from trust barriers requires courage, self-awareness, and a commitment to personal and team growth. By addressing and processing emotional baggage, you pave the way for stronger connections, improved communication, and enhanced collaboration within your business, leading to greater success and employee satisfaction. Remember, the journey towards building trust is ongoing, and each step you take is a valuable investment in your leadership and your team's well-being.

By understanding the roots of doubt and distrust, we gain the power to break free from their grasp and embrace vulnerability as a pathway to authentic connections. By exploring the intricacies of communication, transparency, and cultural influences, we equip ourselves with the tools to overcome trust barriers in various settings. As we navigate the complexities of personal and collective obstacles, we open the door to transformative experiences, fostering a culture of trust that ripples through our lives and communities, ultimately leading us towards a more compassionate, connected, and trusting world.

BUILDING BRIDGES: STRATEGIES TO OVERCOME FEAR, SKEPTICISM, AND PAST EXPERIENCES

Now, we will delve into a treasure trove of strategies to build bridges to overcome fear, skepticism, and the lingering effects of past experiences. By exploring these powerful approaches, we empower ourselves and others to break down trust barriers and create a culture of openness, understanding, and trustworthiness. These strategies act as transformative tools, guiding us toward healing, growth, and authentic connection.

In the journey towards building trust and fostering transformative relationships, individuals and organizations often encounter obstacles that can impede progress. Fear, skepticism, and past negative experiences can create barriers, hindering the development of meaningful connections and limiting the potential for growth. However, by proactively implementing strategies to address these challenges, we can build bridges that pave the way for trust and transformation to flourish.

1. Understanding Fear and its Impact: Fear is a powerful emotion that can paralyze individuals and organizations, preventing you from taking risks and embracing new opportunities. It stems from a variety of sources, such as fear of failure, fear of rejection, or fear of the unknown.

Understanding the root causes of fear is crucial to overcoming it. Recognizing that fear is a natural response to change and uncertainty can help you navigate your emotions more effectively.

2. Cultivating Psychological Safety: Creating a psychologically safe environment is essential for overcoming fear and skepticism. When individuals feel psychologically safe, they are more likely to take risks, share ideas, and express their concerns without fear of negative consequences. You and team members must foster a culture of trust, respect, and empathy, where individuals feel valued and supported.

3. Communicating Openly and Transparently: Transparent communication is key to addressing skepticism and dispelling doubts. Openly sharing information about decisions, strategies, and objectives helps build trust and reduces uncertainty. When you have access to accurate and timely information, they are better equipped to understand the rationale behind decisions and can align their actions accordingly.

4. Acknowledging and Validating Past Experiences: Past negative experiences can leave lasting emotional scars that influence present perceptions and interactions. Acknowledging and validating these experiences is essential in creating a safe space for individuals to express their concerns and anxieties. You and team members must demonstrate empathy and actively listen to the experiences and emotions of others.

5. Emphasizing Small Wins: Overcoming fear and skepticism can be a gradual process.

Emphasizing and celebrating small wins along the way can boost morale and reinforce the belief that positive change is possible. Recognizing and celebrating progress, no matter how incremental, encourages individuals to stay committed to the transformation journey.

6. Encouraging Risk-Taking and Innovation: Fear and skepticism can stifle creativity and innovation. Encouraging a culture that values experimentation and risk-taking can help individuals overcome their fears of failure. You should provide the necessary support and resources to empower individuals to take calculated risks and pursue innovative solutions.

7. Building Trust Through Action: Trust is built through actions, not just words. Leaders and team members must demonstrate consistency in their behavior and follow through on commitments. By aligning words with actions, individuals can build credibility and trust, encouraging others to embrace the transformational journey.

8. Offering Support and Resources: Overcoming fear, skepticism, and past negative experiences often requires support and resources. Providing access to training, coaching, or counseling can help individuals address their fears and build the necessary skills and resilience to navigate challenges.

9. Empowering Inclusivity and Diverse Perspectives: Embracing diverse perspectives and inclusivity can challenge preconceived notions and broaden individuals' understanding of different experiences. By seeking input from diverse voices, organizations can foster an environment that values differing viewpoints and creates a richer tapestry of ideas.

10. Fostering a Learning Culture: Embracing a learning culture encourages individuals to view failures and setbacks as opportunities for growth and improvement. Encouraging continuous learning and development can help individuals overcome the fear of making mistakes and foster a growth mindset.

11. Practicing Empathy and Compassion: Fear and skepticism often arise from feeling misunderstood or unheard. Practicing empathy and compassion allows individuals to connect on a deeper level and build trust. Demonstrating genuine care for others' well-being creates a supportive environment where individuals feel comfortable sharing their concerns.

12. Celebrating Vulnerability and Resilience:

Acknowledging vulnerability as a strength rather than a weakness can empower individuals to overcome their fears. Celebrating acts of vulnerability and resilience fosters a culture where individuals are encouraged to take risks and learn from their experiences.

13. Setting Realistic Expectations:

Overcoming fear, skepticism, and past negative experiences is a journey that takes time and effort. Setting realistic expectations for the transformation process helps individuals stay committed and motivated. Recognizing that transformation is a gradual process enables individuals to navigate challenges with patience and perseverance.

14.   Seeking   Supportive   Networks: Surrounding oneself with supportive networks and mentors can provide encouragement and guidance. Seeking advice and mentorship from individuals who have successfully navigated similar challenges can offer valuable insights and inspiration.

15. Emphasizing the Bigger Purpose: Keeping sight of the bigger purpose and the positive impact of transformation can help individuals overcome their fears and doubts. By reminding themselves of the greater good that comes from embracing change, individuals can find the motivation to push past obstacles.

Overcoming fear, skepticism, and past negative experiences requires a concerted effort from individuals and organizations alike. By implementing these strategies and building bridges of trust and understanding, individuals can embark on a transformative journey that leads to growth, innovation, and lasting positive change. Remember, transformation is not a destination but a continuous process, and with resilience, courage, and a commitment to open-mindedness, the barriers to trust and transformation can be dismantled, allowing for profound personal and organizational growth.

- **Transparency and Honesty: The Pillars of Trust**

Transparency and honesty are the pillars upon which trust is built. In the business world, being truthful and forthcoming in your actions and communications is a powerful way to cultivate trust and dispel doubt among your team and stakeholders.

When you prioritize honesty and transparency, you build a solid foundation of trust that can lead to increased employee engagement, improved relationships with customers, and enhanced business success. Here's why being truthful and forthcoming is essential:

1. Building Credibility:

When you consistently demonstrate honesty and transparency in your actions and communications, you establish credibility as a leader. Your team and stakeholders know that they can rely on your word and trust that you will follow through on your commitments. Credibility is crucial for gaining support, loyalty, and respect, which are essential for effective leadership.

2. Fostering Open Communication:

Being truthful and forthcoming encourages open communication within your organization. When team members feel that they can share their ideas, concerns, and feedback without fear of repercussions, it creates a culture of trust and psychological safety. Open communication leads to better problem-solving, innovation, and collaboration, driving your business forward.

3. Strengthening Relationships:

Trust is the bedrock of strong relationships in business. When you are truthful and forthcoming, you demonstrate that you value and respect your team and stakeholders. This strengthens the bond between you and them, leading to more meaningful and productive interactions. Strong relationships lead to increased loyalty, which is crucial for employee retention and customer satisfaction.

4. Resolving Conflicts and Issues:

In a business environment, conflicts and issues are inevitable. However, when you prioritize honesty and transparency, you can address these challenges more effectively. Openly communicating about problems and finding solutions together builds trust and ensures that issues are resolved in a fair and collaborative manner.

5. Building Customer Loyalty:

Customers appreciate honesty and transparency from businesses. When you are truthful about your products, services, and business practices, you build customer loyalty and trust. Being forthcoming about any shortcomings or mistakes also shows that you take responsibility for your actions, further strengthening the bond with your customers.

6. Enhancing Decision-Making:

Honesty and transparency in business lead to better decision-making. When you have access to accurate and reliable information, you can make well-informed choices that benefit the entire organization. Transparent decision-making also fosters a sense of inclusion among your team members, making them more committed to the outcomes.

7. Creating a Positive Reputation:

In today's digital age, information spreads quickly. By being truthful and forthcoming, you can build a positive reputation for your business. Trustworthy businesses are more likely to attract top talent, investors, and loyal customers, all of which contribute to long-term success.

In summary, being truthful and forthcoming in your actions and communications is a fundamental aspect of effective leadership and business success. By prioritizing honesty and transparency, you cultivate trust among your team and stakeholders, foster open communication, and strengthen relationships.

This trust and credibility extend to your customers, enhancing loyalty and reputation. As a leader, embracing honesty and transparency will not only dispel doubt but also empower your business to thrive and excel in a competitive marketplace. Remember, trust is earned through consistent actions, and once established, it becomes a powerful asset that can propel your business to new heights.

- **Communicating Boundaries: Respecting Individuality**

Clear communication of boundaries is essential in overcoming trust barriers. In the business world, expressing and respecting personal boundaries is crucial for fostering trust and creating a safe space for meaningful connections with your colleagues, clients, and stakeholders.

Setting clear and healthy boundaries allows you to establish a professional environment where everyone feels valued, respected, and understood. Here's how expressing and respecting personal boundaries can positively impact your business relationships and overall success:

1. Building Trust:

When you communicate your personal boundaries to others in a professional manner, it shows that you are confident and assertive in defining your needs and limitations. This openness fosters trust among your colleagues and clients, as they see you as someone who is honest, reliable, and true to your word. Trust is the foundation of successful business relationships and partnerships.

2. Establishing Respectful Communication:

Expressing your personal boundaries in a business setting promotes clear and respectful communication. By setting limits on what you are comfortable with and being receptive to others' boundaries, you create an environment where ideas, feedback, and concerns can be openly discussed without fear of judgment or conflict.

3. Strengthening Collaboration:

Respecting personal boundaries is vital for fostering effective collaboration within teams and across departments. When team members feel their boundaries are respected, they are more likely to contribute their unique perspectives and expertise, leading to better problem-solving and decision-making processes.

4. Enhancing Productivity and Focus:

Clear personal boundaries help you maintain focus and prioritize tasks effectively. When you communicate your availability and limitations, it prevents others from overwhelming you with unnecessary demands, allowing you to concentrate on the most important aspects of your work.

5. Creating a Supportive Work Environment:

Expressing and respecting personal boundaries promotes a culture of support and understanding. Your colleagues and clients will appreciate your honesty and willingness to accommodate their boundaries, leading to a more positive and inclusive work environment.

6. Reducing Conflict and Misunderstandings:

Miscommunication and conflicts often arise when personal boundaries are not clearly expressed or respected. By being upfront about your boundaries and listening attentively to others, you can prevent misunderstandings and address any potential conflicts in a constructive manner.

7. Encouraging Work-Life Balance: Setting boundaries is essential for maintaining a healthy work-life balance. By expressing your need for personal time and space, you demonstrate that you value well-being and mental health, setting an example for others to do the same.

8. Strengthening Client Relationships: Clients appreciate when you respect their boundaries and preferences. By understanding their needs and preferences, you can tailor your services or products to meet their specific requirements, leading to stronger client loyalty and long-term partnerships.

In conclusion, expressing and respecting personal boundaries in a business context is a vital aspect of fostering trust and creating a safe space for meaningful connections.

By setting clear limits, promoting open communication, and valuing the boundaries of others, you build a culture of trust, respect, and collaboration in your professional interactions. Embracing personal boundaries not only enhances productivity and teamwork but also contributes to a supportive and harmonious work environment.

As you prioritize and uphold personal boundaries in your business relationships, you'll find that trust deepens, connections grow, and your overall success flourishes. Remember, mutual respect and understanding are the cornerstones of meaningful and enduring business connections.

- **Building Trust in Incremental Steps: Patience and Perseverance**

Building trust is a gradual process that requires patience and perseverance. In the business world, taking small, consistent steps towards trust-building can have a profound impact on your professional relationships and overall success.

Trust is not built overnight; it requires consistent effort and genuine actions over time. By focusing on gradual trust-building, you can lay the foundation for profound transformations in your business interactions. Here's how taking small, consistent steps can lead to significant improvements in your business relationships:

1. Cultivating Reliability:

Consistently delivering on your promises and commitments builds trust in your reliability as a business partner or colleague. When others can count on you to follow through on your words, they feel more confident in collaborating with you and relying on your contributions.

2. Demonstrating Consistency:

Consistency in your behavior and communication fosters trust in your authenticity and professionalism. By being consistently respectful, supportive, and responsive, you demonstrate that you are genuinely invested in the success of your business relationships.

3. Building Rapport:

Engaging in regular, open communication with your colleagues and clients allows you to build rapport and understanding over time. As you share insights, challenges, and successes, you create a sense of camaraderie that strengthens the foundation of trust.

4. Valuing Feedback:

Actively seeking and appreciating feedback from others shows that you value their perspectives and are willing to improve. Responding positively to feedback and making necessary adjustments conveys your commitment to continuous growth and improvement.

5. Honoring Commitments:

Being true to your word and honoring your commitments, no matter how small, reflects your integrity and builds trust in your character. People feel more at ease working with someone they can rely on to act ethically and professionally.

6. Empowering Others:

Encouraging and supporting the growth and success of your colleagues and team members establishes a culture of trust and collaboration. As you empower others to shine, you create an environment where everyone feels valued and motivated to contribute their best.

7. Acknowledging Mistakes:

Admitting mistakes and taking responsibility for them demonstrates humility and authenticity. When you acknowledge and learn from your errors, you show that you are committed to personal and professional growth, fostering trust in your ability to handle challenges.

8. Offering Help and Support:

Being consistently available to offer help and support when needed reinforces the idea that you are a reliable and dependable colleague or partner. Your willingness to lend a hand builds trust in your commitment to teamwork and collective success.

9. Celebrating Successes:

Recognizing and celebrating individual and team achievements reinforces a positive and supportive work environment. Acknowledging successes fosters a sense of appreciation and trust among team members, inspiring continued collaboration and dedication.

In conclusion, taking small, consistent steps towards trust-building in the business context can lead to profound transformations over time. By cultivating reliability, demonstrating consistency, building rapport, and valuing feedback, you create an environment where trust thrives.

Honoring commitments, empowering others, acknowledging mistakes, and offering help and support further solidify the trust you've built. As you celebrate successes and foster a positive work environment, the profound impact of trust on your professional relationships becomes evident.

Embracing a steady and intentional approach to trust-building paves the way for lasting and meaningful transformations in your business interactions, leading to enhanced collaboration, productivity, and success. Remember, trust is a powerful currency in the business world, and the small steps you take today can make a significant difference in building lasting trust and achieving remarkable outcomes in the future.

These powerful tools enable us to navigate the complexities of trust-building, fostering a culture of openness, understanding, and vulnerability. Through self-awareness, empathy, and active listening, we create a foundation for authentic connections, dissolving skepticism, and fostering mutual trust.

By embracing forgiveness, honesty, and transparency, we pave the way for healing and transformation, breaking free from the barriers that hinder personal and collective growth. As we embrace these strategies, we become architects of trust, bridging the gaps that separate us and cultivating a world where trust ripples through our interactions, paving the way for positive change and uniting us as a global community based on mutual respect and genuine connections.

TRUST IN A DISTRUSTING WORLD: REBUILDING FAITH IN A SOCIETY PLAGUED BY DISTRUST

In a world where distrust seems to be on the rise, rebuilding faith and fostering trust have become vital pursuits for individuals, communities, and societies as a whole. Widespread mistrust can permeate every aspect of life, from personal relationships to institutions, and even affect social cohesion. The erosion of trust can lead to a breakdown in communication, hinder cooperation, and impede progress. However, by recognizing the roots of distrust and proactively implementing strategies to rebuild faith, we can navigate through the challenges of a distrustful world and cultivate a more trusting and harmonious society.

1. Understanding the Roots of Distrust: To effectively rebuild faith in a distrustful world, it is crucial to comprehend the underlying factors contributing to widespread skepticism. Historical events, broken promises, dishonesty, and systemic issues can all contribute to the erosion of trust. Identifying these roots allows individuals and communities to address the core issues that have fueled distrust.

2. Embracing Transparency and Openness:
Trust can only flourish in an environment of transparency and openness. Being truthful and forthright in communication helps dispel doubts and builds confidence in individuals and institutions. By consistently providing accurate information and sharing intentions openly, you can establish a foundation of trust that withstands the test of time.

3. Cultivating Empathy and Active Listening:
Empathy is a powerful tool in bridging the gap between people who harbor distrust. By putting yourself in others' shoes and genuinely listening to their perspectives, you demonstrate that you value their feelings and concerns. This fosters an atmosphere of understanding and empathy,

encouraging the exchange of ideas and nurturing trust.

4. Restoring Accountability and Responsibility: Acknowledging past mistakes and taking responsibility for them is crucial in rebuilding faith. Leaders, organizations, and individuals must be willing to own up to their errors and actively work towards rectifying them. By demonstrating accountability, you show that you are committed to making amends and rebuilding trust.

5. Promoting Inclusivity and Diversity: Embracing inclusivity and diversity is essential in a distrustful world. By promoting an environment that values different perspectives, backgrounds, and experiences, you create a space where individuals feel respected and accepted. Inclusive societies tend to be more trusting, as they recognize the worth of every individual.

6. Advocating for Social Cohesion: Fostering social cohesion brings people together and strengthens trust in communities. Creating opportunities for people to engage in shared experiences, collaborate on common goals, and support one another establishes a sense of unity and belonging. Trust thrives in cohesive environments where individuals feel connected to one another.

7. Addressing Institutional Reforms: Rebuilding faith in institutions often requires significant reforms. Holding institutions accountable, demanding transparency, and advocating for policy changes can help restore trust in those organizations that have been plagued by distrust. Institutional reforms demonstrate a commitment to positive change and can win back public trust.

8. Promoting Media Literacy and Responsible Journalism: In a distrustful world, media literacy is vital. Encouraging critical thinking and responsible journalism helps individuals discern accurate information from misinformation or biased reporting. Educating the public on media literacy empowers them to make informed decisions and fosters a more trustful relationship with the media.

9. Encouraging Ethical Leadership: Ethical leadership is a cornerstone of rebuilding trust in a society plagued by distrust. Leaders who prioritize honesty, integrity, and transparency serve as role models for others. Ethical leaders inspire trust and set a positive example for the rest of society.

10. Fostering a Culture of Trustworthiness: Creating a culture of trustworthiness requires the active participation of individuals at all levels of society. By upholding ethical standards, demonstrating integrity, and valuing honesty, you contribute to a culture where trust can thrive.

11. Investing in Education and Awareness: Investing in education and awareness programs can help instill the importance of trust in future generations. Teaching young individuals the value of trust, integrity, and empathy can contribute to a more trusting and harmonious society in the long run.

12. Bridging Divides and Building Common Ground: In a distrustful world, finding common ground and bridging divides is essential for rebuilding faith. Seeking areas of agreement and focusing on shared goals can help break down barriers and foster cooperation among diverse groups.

13. Celebrating Trustworthy Actions: Acknowledging and celebrating trustworthy actions reinforces positive behavior and promotes a culture of trust. Recognizing individuals and organizations that consistently demonstrate trustworthiness encourages others to follow suit.

14. Resilience in the Face of Setbacks: Rebuilding faith in a distrustful world is not without challenges. There will be setbacks and obstacles along the way. Resilience and determination are vital in navigating through these challenges and remaining committed to the path of rebuilding trust.

15.   Leveraging   Technology   for Trust-building: Technology can play a significant role in rebuilding faith and fostering trust. Utilizing secure and transparent technology platforms can help restore trust in digital interactions and ensure privacy and security.

Rebuilding faith in a society plagued by distrust is an arduous but essential journey. It requires the collective effort of individuals, institutions, and leaders to address the root causes of distrust and implement strategies to foster trust and understanding. By embracing transparency, empathy, inclusivity, and accountability, we can navigate through the challenges of a distrustful world and pave the way for a more trusting and united society.

Rebuilding trust involves collective efforts at the individual, community, and global levels, as we navigate the challenges of the disinformation age and historical injustices. By fostering empathy, promoting critical thinking, and investing in the potential of youth, we create a foundation for a future built on trust, cooperation, and understanding.

As we rebuild faith in a distrusting world, we are reminded of the resilience and hope fueling our commitment to a world where trust becomes the bridge that unites humanity in shared aspirations for a brighter, interconnected future.

PERSONAL GROWTH THROUGH TRUST: EMPOWERING THE JOURNEY OF SELF-DISCOVERY

In the realm of personal development, trust emerges as a potent catalyst, empowering individuals to embark on a transformative journey of self-discovery. The interplay between trust and personal growth nurtures a harmonious relationship, as you, the seeker of self-awareness and empowerment, delve into the depths of trust to unearth the treasures of authenticity and vulnerability.

As you navigate the landscape of personal growth through trust, you unlock the key to unlocking your true potential and embracing the power of self-discovery.

1. The Foundation of Self-Discovery: Personal growth is rooted in self-discovery—the process of exploring the depths of your identity, beliefs, values, and emotions. Trust serves as the fertile soil upon which this foundation is built, creating a safe and nurturing environment for you to embark on this inward journey.

2. Embracing Vulnerability: Trust and vulnerability intertwine on the path of self-discovery. To authentically explore and understand yourself, you must embrace vulnerability—the willingness to open yourself up, exposing your fears, doubts, and insecurities. Trust acts as a gentle guide, reassuring you that it is safe to be vulnerable, fostering an environment free of judgment and criticism.

3. The Trustful Mirror: Trust, like a mirror, reflects your true essence, allowing you to see yourself more clearly. As you delve into self-discovery, the mirror of trust unveils your strengths, passions, and areas for growth, providing an honest reflection of your inner world.

4. Cultivating Self-Compassion: Trust invites self-compassion—a crucial element in the journey of self-discovery. Through trust, you learn to be kind and gentle with yourself, embracing imperfections and setbacks as stepping stones to growth. Self-compassion nurtures resilience, empowering you to persevere through challenges on the path of self-discovery.

5. Unraveling Limiting Beliefs: Trust challenges the grip of limiting beliefs that may hold you back from embracing your true potential. As you trust yourself and others, you begin to question and dismantle these self-imposed barriers, opening the door to new possibilities and growth.

6. The Role of Introspection: Trust nurtures introspection—a process of deep self-reflection and examination. As you trust yourself to delve into your inner landscape, you gain insight into your thoughts, emotions, and desires, paving the way for personal growth and transformation.

7. Building Trust in Relationships: Trusting relationships play a pivotal role in your journey of self-discovery. As you surround yourself with trusted allies—friends, mentors, or coaches—you create a support system that encourages and empowers you to explore your authentic self without fear of judgment.

8. Vulnerability as a Strength: In the context of personal growth, vulnerability emerges as a strength, not a weakness. Trusting yourself to be vulnerable allows you to peel away layers of pretense and masks, revealing the core of who you are, fostering a deeper connection with your authentic self.

9. The Healing Power of Trust: For those who have experienced past betrayals or traumas, trust can act as a healing balm. As you trust yourself to navigate the healing process, you begin to mend wounds, rebuilding a stronger sense of self and inner resilience.

10. Embracing Change: Trust empowers you to embrace change as an inevitable part of the self-discovery journey. Rather than fearing change, you trust yourself to adapt and grow through life's transitions, viewing them as opportunities for self-exploration and growth.

11. Trust and Self-Empowerment: Trust nurtures self-empowerment—the sense of being in control of your life and choices. As you trust yourself to make decisions aligned with your values and aspirations, you step into the driver's seat of your personal growth journey.

12. Finding Clarity and Purpose: Trusting in the process of self-discovery allows you to find clarity and purpose in life. The trustful journey guides you to uncover your passions, interests, and aspirations, helping you align your actions with your authentic self.

13. Celebrating Progress: Trust encourages you to celebrate every step forward on your journey of self-discovery. Each moment of growth, no matter how small, deserves acknowledgment and appreciation, reinforcing your sense of accomplishment and self-worth.

14. Trusting the Unknown: Self-discovery often leads to uncharted territories, inviting you to trust the unknown. As you venture beyond your comfort zone, you trust yourself to navigate uncertainty and embrace the growth opportunities it presents.

15. The Pyramid Trust: Personal growth through trust creates a pyramid trust, impacting your relationships, work, and overall well-being. As you embrace vulnerability and authenticity, you inspire others to do the same, contributing to a more trusting and empowered community.

16. Embodying Trust in Leadership: As a leader of your own life, trust plays a critical role in your ability to lead and influence others positively. Trusting your own capabilities and leading by example empowers you to inspire trust in others, creating a supportive and growth-oriented environment.

17. Nurturing Continuous Growth: Trust and self-discovery form a symbiotic relationship, nurturing continuous growth. The journey of self-discovery deepens your trust in yourself, while trust empowers you to continue exploring new dimensions of self-awareness.

18. Trust as a Lifelong Companion: Personal growth through trust is a lifelong endeavor. The trustful mirror accompanies you throughout your life, reflecting your growth, resilience, and the profound transformation that occurs through self-discovery.

In conclusion, personal growth through trust embodies a transformative and empowering journey of self-discovery. Trust acts as the guiding compass, allowing you to navigate the depths of vulnerability and authenticity.. By embracing trust as a guiding principle in our relationships with ourselves and others, we unlock the door to a profound journey of self-awareness, resilience, and empowerment. Through nurturing trust within, we discover our authentic selves, build self-confidence, and unleash our potential for positive change.

The trustful mirror reflects the multifaceted dimensions of your identity, guiding you on an ever-evolving path of growth and transformation. As you continue to trust the process of self-discovery, you empower yourself to rewrite your narrative, embracing a life enriched by trust, authenticity, and purpose.

- **Trust as a Mirror: Reflecting Authenticity**

The trust serves as a mirror, reflecting our authentic selves to us. In the intricate web of human connections, trust emerges as a powerful and essential element that underpins our interactions, shaping the quality of our relationships, both personal and professional.

Like a mirror, trust reflects the true essence of these bonds, revealing the depth of authenticity and vulnerability present within them. Trust as a mirror is a profound concept that illuminates the mutual exchange of emotions, beliefs, and intentions between individuals, creating a safe and transformative space for meaningful connections to thrive.

1. The Reflective Nature of Trust: Trust functions as a mirror that reflects the true nature of our relationships. It allows us to see ourselves and others more clearly, unveiling both strengths and vulnerabilities. As trust deepens, this mirror becomes clearer, providing an honest reflection of the dynamics at play within the relationship.

2. Vulnerability and Trust: Trust and vulnerability share an intrinsic relationship. For trust to take root, individuals must be willing to open themselves up, embracing vulnerability and revealing their authentic selves. This act of vulnerability creates a safe space where trust can flourish, fostering deeper emotional connections and understanding.

3. Building the Trustful Mirror: Establishing trust requires consistent effort and genuine intentions. As you interact with others, your actions and words are reflected in the trustful mirror. Demonstrating integrity, honesty, and reliability builds a positive reflection, strengthening the bond of trust.

4. Repairing Broken Mirrors: Trust, like a mirror, can be fragile. When it is broken, it may shatter into pieces, leaving scars on the relationship. Repairing the trustful mirror calls for humility and accountability. Acknowledging past missteps, offering sincere apologies, and taking actions to rebuild trust are essential steps in repairing the mirror's cracks.

5. The Role of Communication: Communication acts as a polishing agent for the trustful mirror. Open and transparent communication clears away any smudges or distortions, ensuring a clear reflection of intentions and emotions. Active listening and empathy play a pivotal role in fine-tuning the mirror, enabling you to understand others deeply.

6. Trust's Influence on Self-Perception: Trust not only reflects the nature of our relationships with others but also impacts how we see ourselves. When others trust us, it reinforces a positive self-perception, fostering self-confidence and a sense of worthiness. Conversely, a lack of trust may lead to self-doubt and insecurity.

7. Cultivating Empathy and Understanding: Empathy acts as a magnifying glass for the trustful mirror, enhancing its ability to reflect emotions and feelings. By genuinely understanding others' perspectives, you strengthen the mirror's clarity, promoting an atmosphere of trust and compassion.

8. Trust and Team Dynamics: In the realm of business and leadership, trust plays a pivotal role in team dynamics. As you lead a team, trust acts as a cohesive force, reflecting the level of confidence team members have in each other and in you as their leader. A high level of trust fosters collaboration, innovation, and productivity.

9. Trust's Pyramid Trust: The trustful mirror's impact extends beyond individual relationships. Trust has a pyramid effect, spreading from one connection to another, creating a network of trust within teams, organizations, and even society as a whole. The pyramid trust demonstrates how trust can transform entire communities and institutions.

10. The Vulnerable Leader: As a leader, embracing vulnerability and transparency allows the trustful mirror to reflect your authenticity. Sharing your challenges and growth creates a relatable and approachable image, encouraging trust among your team members. A vulnerable leader leads by example, inspiring others to be open and trustworthy.

11. Nurturing Trust in a Distrusting World: In a world often plagued by distrust, nurturing trust becomes an indispensable task. The trustful mirror can be a guiding light in rebuilding faith and fostering understanding among diverse communities. By actively working to cultivate trust, you contribute to a more harmonious and empathetic society.

12. The Long-Term Nature of Trust: Trust, like a mirror, evolves over time. It requires patience and consistent effort to maintain its clarity. As you invest in building trust, the mirror's reflection deepens, revealing the profound connections and growth that develop within authentic relationships.

13. Trust and Resilience: A strong foundation of trust enhances resilience in relationships and organizations. When challenges arise, the trustful mirror reflects the ability to weather storms together, fostering unity and cohesion in times of adversity.

14. Trust's Intersection with Forgiveness: Trust and forgiveness are intertwined, with forgiveness acting as a cleansing agent for the trustful mirror. When we forgive past transgressions, we allow the mirror to clear any lingering shadows, paving the way for renewed trust and healing.

15. The Trustful Journey: Trust, as a mirror, guides us on a transformative journey. As you engage in open and vulnerable connections, the mirror reflects the growth and evolution of your relationships. Each step on this journey nurtures trust and reveals the depths of meaningful connections.

16. The Mirror of Introspection: Trust also invites introspection. Gazing into the trustful mirror prompts self-reflection, enabling you to assess your own trustworthiness and areas for growth. Honest self-evaluation contributes to personal development and the cultivation of stronger relationships.

17. Trust's Legacy: Trust's legacy endures beyond individual encounters. The positive reflection in the trustful mirror leaves an indelible impact on the lives of those you connect with, inspiring them to embrace trust in their own relationships and interactions.

18. The Transformative Power of Trust: Ultimately, trust as a mirror is a testament to the transformative power of authentic relationships. It serves as a reminder that trust is not a stagnant concept but an ever-evolving force that deepens with time, love, and vulnerability.

In conclusion, trust as a mirror is a profound metaphor that reminds us of the beauty and complexity of human connections. By recognizing the reflective nature of trust, nurturing vulnerability, and fostering open communication, we can cultivate stronger, more authentic relationships in both our personal and professional lives. The trustful mirror invites us to embark on a journey of growth, healing, and transformation, as we navigate the intricacies of trust in a world marked by skepticism and doubt. As you look into the mirror of trust, you discover the profound impact your actions and intentions have on others, encouraging you to embody trust and empathy as you navigate through life's intricate tapestry of relationships.

By embracing trust as a guiding principle in our relationship with ourselves and others, we unlock the door to self-awareness, resilience, and authenticity. Trust becomes the mirror that reflects our authentic selves, empowering us to embrace vulnerability, step into the unknown, and unleash our true potential.

We learn to trust our intuition, navigate uncertainties, and build self-confidence as we honor our growth process with patience and self-compassion. By surrounding ourselves with trustworthy and supportive connections, we create an environment that nurtures our personal growth and sense of belonging.

As we cultivate trust in our abilities, potential, and capacity for change, we unlock a world of possibilities, embracing each step of our journey of self-discovery with authenticity and a growth mindset. Ultimately, through the power of trust, we discover the profound depths of our true selves, unleashing the transformative potential within us, and becoming catalysts for positive change in our lives and the world around us.

CHAPTER 8

CUSTOMER TRUST: THE HEART OF THRIVING BUSINESSES

In this chapter, we delve into the central role of customer trust in the success and sustainability of businesses. Customer trust forms the foundation of enduring relationships between businesses and their clientele, driving loyalty, advocacy, and long-term success. By exploring the profound impact of trust on customer satisfaction and brand reputation, we uncover the strategies that businesses can employ to cultivate and nurture customer trust, ultimately building a loyal customer base that becomes the lifeblood of thriving enterprises.

In today's competitive marketplace, building a strong and enduring customer-brand connection is essential for business success. As you, the business leader, embark on the journey of nurturing trust and loyalty with your customers, you set the stage for long-term relationships that go beyond transactions. In this comprehensive exploration of the customer-brand connection, we delve into the multifaceted dimensions of trust and loyalty, uncovering the strategies and practices that will elevate your brand to new heights of customer satisfaction and advocacy.

1. Understanding the Foundation of Trust: Trust is the bedrock of the customer-brand connection. As you foster trust with your customers, you demonstrate your commitment to delivering on promises, providing reliable products or services, and being transparent in your business practices. Trust acts as the glue that binds customers to your brand, ensuring repeat business and positive word-of-mouth referrals.

2. Delivering Consistent Value: Customers seek consistent value from the brands they interact with. By consistently providing products or services that meet or exceed customer expectations, you build a track record of dependability and reliability. Consistency is key to gaining trust and fostering customer loyalty, as customers come to rely on your brand to fulfill their needs and desires.

3. Building Authenticity and Transparency: In a world saturated with marketing messages, authenticity and transparency stand out as cornerstones of trust. When you communicate openly and honestly with your customers, you create an environment of mutual respect and understanding. As customers perceive your brand as authentic, they are more likely to trust in your intentions and align with your values.

4. Personalizing the Customer Experience: Emphasizing personalization in the customer journey deepens the emotional connection between your brand and your customers. By tailoring interactions based on customer preferences, needs, and behavior, you demonstrate that you value them as individuals. Personalization evokes a sense of being understood and cared for, reinforcing trust and loyalty.

5. Empowering Customer Feedback and Engagement: Trust is fortified when you actively seek and listen to customer feedback. By providing channels for customers to voice their opinions and concerns, you show that their satisfaction matters. Addressing feedback promptly and genuinely demonstrates your commitment to continuous improvement and customer-centricity.

6. Consistency in Brand Messaging: A consistent brand message across all touchpoints reinforces the image of your brand in the minds of customers. Cohesive branding builds recognition and trust, as customers come to associate your brand with a specific set of values, qualities, and benefits.

7. Embracing Customer-Centricity: Placing the customer at the heart of your business decisions signifies a genuine commitment to their needs. As you prioritize customer-centricity, you ensure that your products, services, and marketing efforts align with what your customers truly value, fostering trust and loyalty.

8. Honoring Promises and Guarantees: Upholding promises and guarantees is paramount in nurturing trust and loyalty. When you deliver on your commitments, customers feel secure in their choices and are more likely to engage with your brand in the long run.

9. Leveraging Social Proof: Positive customer reviews and testimonials serve as social proof of your brand's credibility. Sharing these testimonials with your audience reinforces trust in your brand, as potential customers see that others have had positive experiences with your offerings.

10. Empathy and Understanding: Demonstrating empathy and understanding in your customer interactions goes a long way in building trust. As you put yourself in your customers' shoes, you can better address their needs and concerns, fostering a sense of care and empathy that strengthens the customer-brand connection.

11. Addressing Customer Concerns Proactively: Addressing customer concerns promptly and proactively shows your dedication to their satisfaction. By resolving issues with empathy and efficiency, you demonstrate that you value their time and trust in your brand.

12. Creating Delightful Experiences: Going above and beyond to create delightful customer experiences cements the bond between your brand and your customers. Surprising and delighting customers through personalized gestures or unexpected perks leaves a lasting impression, cultivating loyalty and advocacy.

13. Aligning with Customer Values: Understanding and aligning with your customers' values and beliefs fosters a sense of shared purpose. When your brand stands for something meaningful to your customers, you forge a deeper emotional connection, leading to heightened loyalty and support.

14. Cultivating a Community: Creating a community around your brand fosters a sense of belonging and kinship among your customers.

Through online forums, social media groups, or exclusive events, you provide a platform for customers to connect with one another and with your brand, enhancing trust and loyalty.

15. Rewarding Loyalty: Acknowledging and rewarding loyal customers not only shows appreciation but also incentivizes repeat business. Loyalty programs, special discounts, or exclusive access to new products or services are all ways to reinforce loyalty and encourage further engagement.

16. Celebrating Milestones Together: Celebrating milestones, both for your brand and your customers, brings you closer together. By acknowledging and commemorating important events, achievements, or anniversaries, you express gratitude for their support, deepening the sense of connection.

17. Adapting to Evolving Customer Needs: As customer needs evolve, so must your brand. Remaining agile and responsive to changing market demands and customer preferences demonstrates your commitment to meeting their evolving expectations, nurturing trust and loyalty.

18. The Trust-Loyalty Loop: Trust and loyalty create a virtuous cycle—a trust-loyalty loop. As customers trust your brand, they become more loyal, leading to increased customer retention and advocacy. In turn, loyal customers reinforce the trust of potential customers through positive word-of-mouth.

19. Data Security and Privacy: In the digital age, data security and privacy are paramount concerns for customers. By prioritizing robust security measures and respecting customer privacy, you create a sense of safety and trust in your brand's digital interactions.

20. Embracing Innovation Responsibly: Innovation can be a powerful driver of trust and loyalty when executed responsibly. Introducing new technologies or features that enhance the customer experience demonstrates your dedication to continuous improvement and customer-centricity.

In conclusion, the customer-brand connection is a dynamic relationship founded on trust and loyalty. As you, the leader, prioritize building trust with your customers through authenticity, transparency, and customer-centric practices, you create a solid foundation for lasting loyalty and advocacy. By consistently delivering value, understanding and meeting customer needs, and fostering personalized, delightful experiences, you nurture a loyal customer base that remains steadfast through various market challenges. The unwavering connection between your brand and your customers forms the heart of your business's success, driving growth, and empowering your brand to thrive in a competitive landscape.

KEEPING PROMISES: DELIVERING ON COMMITMENTS FOR LASTING CUSTOMER RELATIONSHIPS

In the competitive business landscape, promises are more than mere words; they are the foundation upon which lasting customer relationships are built. As you, the leader, seek to create a loyal customer base, the ability to keep promises and deliver on commitments becomes paramount. In this extensive exploration, we delve into the significance of keeping promises, how it influences customer perceptions, and the strategies to ensure unwavering commitment to delivering exceptional customer experiences.

1. The Power of Promises: Promises act as a contract between your brand and your customers, setting expectations for the value they will receive from your products or services. Keeping promises establishes credibility and builds trust, providing customers with the assurance that you will deliver on your word.

2. Building Trust through Reliability: As you consistently fulfill your commitments, customers develop a sense of reliability and dependability in your brand. Reliability breeds trust, enhancing the customer-brand relationship and fostering loyalty.

3. Setting Realistic Expectations: The key to keeping promises lies in setting realistic and achievable expectations. By aligning promises with your brand's capabilities and resources, you avoid overpromising and under delivering, ensuring customer satisfaction.

4. Understanding Customer Needs: A deep understanding of your customers' needs enables you to make promises that resonate with them. When you tailor promises to address specific pain points and desires, customers perceive your brand as attentive and customer-centric.

5. Communication and Transparency: Transparent communication is central to keeping promises. Regularly updating customers on progress, potential delays, or changes in plans demonstrates openness and accountability, reinforcing their trust in your brand.

6. Investing in Resources: To fulfill promises, you must invest in the necessary resources, including skilled personnel, technology, and infrastructure. Adequate resource allocation allows you to meet customer expectations consistently.

7. Delivering on Time, Every Time: Timely delivery is crucial in keeping promises. Meeting deadlines and delivering as expected demonstrate your commitment to customer satisfaction, leaving a positive and lasting impression.

8. Quality as a Promise: Delivering quality products or services is a promise in itself. Striving for excellence in every aspect of your offerings reinforces your dedication to providing value to customers.

9. Handling Challenges and Adversities: Challenges and unforeseen obstacles are inevitable in business. How you address and overcome these hurdles speaks volumes about your brand's integrity and dedication to customer success.

10. Accountability and Ownership: Taking ownership of your promises empowers you to fulfill them diligently. Should any issues arise, demonstrating accountability and taking swift action to resolve them builds trust and loyalty.

11. Listening to Customer Feedback: Customer feedback is a valuable tool in refining your promises. Actively listening to customer opinions and incorporating their suggestions enhances the relevance and impact of your commitments.

12. Going Above and Beyond: Exceeding customer expectations whenever possible leaves a lasting impression. Going above and beyond your promises showcases your brand's commitment to customer delight.

13. Reinforcing Promises through Guarantees: Offering guarantees for your products or services bolsters customer confidence. Guarantees provide reassurance that you stand behind your promises, even if unforeseen issues arise.

14. Empowering Customer Service: Your customer service team plays a vital role in keeping promises. Equipping them with the tools and authority to address customer concerns promptly and effectively strengthens trust.

15. Learning from Mistakes: In the pursuit of perfection, mistakes may occur. Embracing mistakes as opportunities for improvement, learning, and growth demonstrates humility and fosters trust.

16. Adapting to Changing Circumstances: The business landscape is dynamic, and circumstances may evolve. Adapting your promises and strategies in response to changes showcases your agility and dedication to customer success.

17. Celebrating Promise Fulfillment: Celebrating successful promise fulfillment reinforces the importance of keeping commitments within your organization. Recognizing teams and individuals who exemplify this dedication nurtures a culture of reliability and accountability.

18. Reinforcing Brand Values: Promises aligned with your brand values resonate with customers on a deeper level. Consistently upholding these values through promises and actions reinforces your brand's identity and purpose.

19. Building Long-Term Partnerships: Keeping promises fosters long-term partnerships with customers. Long-term customers become brand advocates, spreading positive word-of-mouth and contributing to sustainable business growth.

20. Cultivating a Promise-Driven Culture: Infusing your organization with a promise-driven culture reinforces the significance of delivering on commitments. A culture that values and prioritizes keeping promises sets the stage for lasting customer relationships.

In conclusion, keeping promises is the cornerstone of lasting customer relationships. As you, the leader, commit to delivering on your word and building trust through reliability, transparency, and customer-centricity, you create a customer base that remains loyal and devoted to your brand.

Embracing challenges with accountability and learning from mistakes reinforces your brand's authenticity and fosters trust. Remember, every promise fulfilled paves the way for a stronger and more prosperous future, where your customers become the most fervent advocates of your brand.

REDEMPTION ROAD: REBUILDING TRUST AFTER CUSTOMER GRIEVANCES

In the competitive business landscape, promises are more than mere words; they are the foundation upon which lasting customer relationships are built. As you, the leader, seek to create a loyal customer base, the ability to keep promises and deliver on commitments becomes paramount. In this extensive exploration, we delve into the significance of keeping promises, how it influences customer perceptions, and the strategies to ensure unwavering commitment to delivering exceptional customer experiences.

1. The Power of Promises: Promises act as a contract between your brand and your customers, setting expectations for the value they will receive from your products or services. Keeping promises establishes credibility and builds trust, providing customers with the assurance that you will deliver on your word.

2. Building Trust through Reliability: As you consistently fulfill your commitments, customers develop a sense of reliability and dependability in your brand. Reliability breeds trust, enhancing the customer-brand relationship and fostering loyalty.

3. Setting Realistic Expectations: The key to keeping promises lies in setting realistic and achievable expectations. By aligning promises with your brand's capabilities and resources, you avoid overpromising and under delivering, ensuring customer satisfaction.

4. Understanding Customer Needs: A deep understanding of your customers' needs enables you to make promises that resonate with them. When you tailor promises to address specific pain points and desires, customers perceive your brand as attentive and customer-centric.

5. Communication and Transparency: Transparent communication is central to keeping promises. Regularly updating customers on progress, potential delays, or changes in plans demonstrates openness and accountability, reinforcing their trust in your brand.

6. Investing in Resources: To fulfill promises, you must invest in the necessary resources, including skilled personnel, technology, and infrastructure. Adequate resource allocation allows you to meet customer expectations consistently.

7. Delivering on Time, Every Time: Timely delivery is crucial in keeping promises. Meeting deadlines and delivering as expected demonstrate your commitment to customer satisfaction, leaving a positive and lasting impression.

8. Quality as a Promise: Delivering quality products or services is a promise in itself. Striving for excellence in every aspect of your offerings reinforces your dedication to providing value to customers.

9. Handling Challenges and Adversities: Challenges and unforeseen obstacles are inevitable in business. How you address and overcome these hurdles speaks volumes about your brand's integrity and dedication to customer success.

10. Accountability and Ownership: Taking ownership of your promises empowers you to fulfill them diligently. Should any issues arise, demonstrating accountability and taking swift action to resolve them builds trust and loyalty.

11. Listening to Customer Feedback: Customer feedback is a valuable tool in refining your promises. Actively listening to customer opinions and incorporating their suggestions enhances the relevance and impact of your commitments.

12. Going Above and Beyond: Exceeding customer expectations whenever possible leaves a lasting impression. Going above and beyond your promises showcases your brand's commitment to customer delight.

13. Reinforcing Promises through Guarantees: Offering guarantees for your products or services bolsters customer confidence. Guarantees provide reassurance that you stand behind your promises, even if unforeseen issues arise.

14. Empowering Customer Service: Your customer service team plays a vital role in keeping promises. Equipping them with the tools and authority to address customer concerns promptly and effectively strengthens trust.

15. Learning from Mistakes: In the pursuit of perfection, mistakes may occur. Embracing mistakes as opportunities for improvement, learning, and growth demonstrates humility and fosters trust.

16. Adapting to Changing Circumstances: The business landscape is dynamic, and circumstances may evolve. Adapting your promises and strategies in response to changes showcases your agility and dedication to customer success.

17. Celebrating Promise Fulfillment: Celebrating successful promise fulfillment reinforces the importance of keeping commitments within your organization. Recognizing teams and individuals who exemplify this dedication nurtures a culture of reliability and accountability.

18. Reinforcing Brand Values: Promises aligned with your brand values resonate with customers on a deeper level. Consistently upholding these values through promises and actions reinforces your brand's identity and purpose.

19. Building Long-Term Partnerships: Keeping promises fosters long-term partnerships with customers. Long-term customers become brand advocates, spreading positive word-of-mouth and contributing to sustainable business growth.

20. Cultivating a Promise-Driven Culture: Infusing your organization with a promise-driven culture reinforces the significance of delivering on commitments. A culture that values and prioritizes keeping promises sets the stage for lasting customer relationships.

In conclusion, keeping promises is the cornerstone of lasting customer relationships. As you, the leader, commit to delivering on your word and building trust through reliability, transparency, and customer-centricity, you create a customer base that remains loyal and devoted to your brand. By setting realistic expectations, communicating openly, and investing in resources to fulfill promises, you demonstrate your dedication to customer satisfaction and success.

Embracing challenges with accountability and learning from mistakes reinforces your brand's authenticity and fosters trust. Remember, every promise fulfilled paves the way for a stronger and more prosperous future, where your customers become the most fervent advocates of your brand.

CONCLUSION

As we reach the culmination of this profound exploration, The Pyramid Trust emerges as a beacon of hope and transformation. Throughout the pages of this book, we've unraveled the intricate dimensions of trust and its unwavering power in shaping our lives, relationships, and organizations.

Trust stands as the cornerstone of authentic connections, and as we've witnessed, it acts as the catalyst for positive change and lasting transformation. It unlocks the potential within individuals and empowers teams to achieve greatness. It fosters a culture of belief, where individuals thrive, and organizations flourish.

Embracing the pyramid trust is not just an intellectual endeavor; it's an invitation to action. As you close this chapter, you are invited to embark on a personal journey of trust. In your personal relationships, be vulnerable and courageous, for trust emerges from the heart's embrace of authenticity.

In the professional realm, prioritize trust in leadership, for it is the bedrock upon which effective leadership is built. Nurture trust within teams, and watch collaboration and performance soar to new heights.

The trust crisis may loom large in the modern business landscape, but you have the power to rekindle the flame. Lead by example, and let trust guide you through uncharted waters, weathering storms of change with grace and adaptability.

Let The Pyramid Trust extend beyond borders, fostering meaningful connections with customers, partners, and communities. In the digital age, leverage technology to create transparent and open channels for trust-building.

So, as you close this book, let the essence of trust linger in your thoughts and actions. Embrace The Pyramid Trust and be the catalyst for transformation in your life and the lives of those around you. As the flame of change ignites within, share your experiences and insights with others, and let your words inspire those on their path of growth and evolution.

Your journey doesn't end here; it's just the beginning. Trust, believe, and embrace the power of transformation through The Pyramid Trust. Your actions, no matter how small, can create a ripple of positive change that extends far beyond what you may imagine.

Thank you for accompanying us on this transformative voyage. Let The Pyramid Trust guide you as you navigate life's challenges, forge meaningful connections, and empower positive change. As we part ways, know that trust remains the key to unlocking the door to a world of endless possibilities.